I0796824

A gift for

....

From

....

Date

....

Hope for Hard Days

90 REFLECTIONS

OF COMFORT, CALM, AND THE CERTAINTY OF HEAVEN

MAX LUCADO

THOMAS NELSON
Since 1798

Hope for Hard Days

Material in this book has been previously published in *Grace for the Moment Volume II* and *What Happens Next.*

Published by Thomas Nelson, 501 Nelson Place, Nashville, TN 37214, USA. Thomas Nelson is a registered trademark of HarperCollins Christian Publishing, Inc.

Thomas Nelson titles may be purchased in bulk for educational, business, fundraising, or sales promotional use. For information, please email SpecialMarkets@ThomasNelson.com.

ISBN 978-1-4002-5646-4 (HC)
ISBN 978-1-4002-5649-5 (audiobook)
ISBN 978-1-4002-5647-1 (e-Book)

HarperCollins Publishers, Macken House, 39/40 Mayor Street Upper, Dublin 1, D01 C9W8, Ireland (https://www.harpercollins.com)

Cover design: Sabryna Lugge
Interior design: Kristy Edwards

Printed in India

26 27 28 29 RPI 10 9 8 7 6 5 4 3

Contents

Introduction

Why talk to God about my troubles? Can he truly understand? According to the Bible, he can: "For we have no superhuman High Priest to whom our weaknesses are unintelligible—he himself has shared fully in all our experience of temptation, except that he never sinned" (Hebrews 4:15 PHILLIPS).

The writer of Hebrews is adamant almost to the point of redundancy. It's as if he anticipates our objections. It's as if he knows that we will say, "God, it's easy for you up there. You don't know how hard it is from down here." So he boldly proclaims Jesus' ability to understand. Look at the wording again.

He himself. Not an angel. Not an ambassador. Not an emissary. But Jesus himself.

Shared fully. Not partially. Not nearly. Not to a large degree. Entirely! Jesus shared fully.

In all our experience. Every hurt. Each ache. All the stresses and all the strains. No exceptions. No substitutes. Why? So he could empathize with our weaknesses.

Every page of the Gospels hammers home this crucial principle: God knows how you feel. From the funeral to the factory to the frustration of a demanding schedule, Jesus understands. When you tell God that you've reached your limit, he knows what you mean. When you shake your head at impossible deadlines, he shakes his too. When your plans are interrupted by people who have other plans, he nods in empathy.

He has been there.

He knows how you feel.

So go ahead and tell him your troubles. Give him your burdens, your worries, and your fears.

Because he himself has shared fully in all our experience.

He is your source of hope, for this life and the next, in all your hard days.

Max

We wait in hope for the LORD; he is our help and our shield.

Psalm 33:20 NIV

Live in the Light

God is light, and in him there is no darkness at all.

1 John 1:5

What if this is as good as it gets?

Many people assume it is. They mistakenly think their fondest moments, deepest joys, and most profound experiences happen sometime between birth and the hearse. Someone needs to tell them the good news: As good as it gets? In no way and by no means. If you are in Christ, this life is as *bad* as it gets.

Every page and every promise of the Bible invites and excites with the lure of a new age and a renewed world. Your best life awaits you!

It only gets better. What's more, we have been handed an itinerary. We know what happens next. Let the promise of the next life define the way you spend this life. Live in the light of heaven.

> When you've been knocked down more times than you can count, when the days are longer and the paychecks are shorter, when tears have etched a pathway from your eyes to your heart, remember . . . this life is as bad as it gets. So hold on. Keep trusting. Keep going. God has something infinitely better waiting for you on the other side of this struggle.

My Scripture of Hope

There will never be night again. They will not need the light of a lamp or the light of the sun, because the Lord God will give them light. And they will rule as kings forever and ever.

REVELATION 22:5

My Hope to Hold On to and My Worries to Release

God's Promise of Hope to Me

One day, darkness will end. Tears will end. Struggles and troubles will end. There will be only God's light, love, joy, and peace. And I will live in it forever . . . *with God.*

My Prayer

DAY 2

Everyday Miracles

The testimony of the Lord is sure, making wise the simple.

Psalm 19:7 NKJV

A small seed becoming a towering tree. A thin stalk pushing back the earth. A rainbow arching in the midst of the thundercloud . . .

"God's testimony," wrote David, "makes wise the simple."

God's testimony. When was the last time you witnessed it? A stroll through knee-high grass in a green meadow. An hour listening to seagulls or looking at seashells on the beach. Or witnessing shafts of sunlight brightening the snow on a crisp winter dawn.

There comes a time when we should lay down our phones and laptops and step out of our offices and libraries. To really understand and believe in the miracle on the cross, we'd do well to witness God's miracles every day.

When was the last time you stepped out of your house, the office, your everyday routine and sought out God's testimony? Take a moment—a bunch of moments—to notice all the declarations of God's presence that fill up your day.

My Scripture of Hope

Through his power all things were made—things in heaven and on earth, things seen and unseen, all powers, authorities, lords, and rulers.

Colossians 1:16

My Hope to Hold On to and My Worries to Release

God's Promise of Hope to Me

I can see the power of God in this world. I can know that he is real and at work by the witness of his creation.

My Prayer

DAY 3

You Can Know the Future

For our present troubles are small and won't last very long. Yet they produce for us a glory that vastly outweighs them and will last forever!
2 CORINTHIANS 4:17 NLT

Hope is an endangered species. We are more troubled than we've been in years. Happiness is down. Loneliness is up. And optimism has taken a right hook to the chin.

You can relate. Your heart has been broken. Your dreams have been shattered. Your body has battled disease and aging. And maybe you've wondered if this life is worth living.

God's therapy for our trepidation reads like this: "For our present troubles are small and won't last very long. Yet they produce for us a glory that vastly outweighs them and will last forever!" (2 Corinthians 4:17 NLT).

Face the problems of this life by focusing on the promises of the next. The future is not as frightening if you know the future. And you can know the future when you know who controls it.

> Troubles don't feel small or short-lived when you're right in the middle of them, do they? But when time is measured against the standard of eternity, they're less than the blink of an eye. God isn't dismissing your problems; rather, he's inviting you to remember that this moment of trouble will be swallowed up by an eternity of wonder. When you need help holding on, remember who holds the future.

My Scripture of Hope

We don't look at the troubles we can see now; rather, we fix our gaze on things that cannot be seen. For the things we see now will soon be gone, but the things we cannot see will last forever.

2 Corinthians 4:18 NLT

My Hope to Hold On to and My Worries to Release

God's Promise of Hope to Me

The struggles and troubles of this world will soon be over. God—his love, his goodness, and my life with him—will last forever.

My Prayer

DAY 4

God Doesn't Remember

I will remember their sins no more.

HEBREWS 8:12 RSV

I was thanking the Father today for his mercy. I began listing the sins he'd forgiven. One by one, I thanked God for forgiving my stumbles and tumbles. My motives were pure, and my heart was thankful, but my understanding of God was wrong. It was when I used the word *remember* that it hit me.

"Remember the time I . . ." I was about to thank God for another act of mercy. But I stopped. Something was wrong. The word *remember* seemed displaced. It didn't fit.

Then *I* remembered. I remembered his words: "I will remember their sins no more."

Wow! Now, *that* is a remarkable promise. God doesn't just forgive; he forgets.

For all the things he does do, this is one thing God refuses to do. He refuses to keep a list of my wrongs.

God refuses to remember the sins he has forgiven. He *chooses* to forget. But do you? Do you allow yourself to forget? Or do you hold on to the sins of the past and let them weigh you down and hold you back? If you've confessed your sin, he has already forgiven you and made you whole. Because he's faithful, you can let it go.

My Scripture of Hope

Though your sins are like scarlet, they shall be as white as snow; though they are red as crimson, they shall be like wool.

Isaiah 1:18 NIV

My Hope to Hold On to and My Worries to Release

God's Promise of Hope to Me

When I take my sins to God, he not only forgives; he also forgets. I can forgive myself and forget those sins too.

My Prayer

DAY 5

You Are Pursued

It is not our love for God; it is God's love for us. He sent his Son to die in our place to take away our sins.

1 JOHN 4:10

In the days of Jesus, it fell to the groom to pursue the bride. She might glance as he passed by, she might smile as he turned, but any initiative for marriage was always taken by the groom. As much as she might long for him, she had no hope of a wedding unless he took the first step.

It's the same for us. Even if we had the charm to entice heaven, we don't know the phone number. If we have any hope of standing at the altar, God must make the call. And he did! He took the first step. He left his house and came to ours.

Jesus is romancing us. Can he exist without us? Of course—but he doesn't want to. He is smitten, captivated, head-over-heels enchanted with us. And he will do whatever it takes to win our affection.

When was the last time you were pursued? When was the last time someone pulled out all the stops to capture your heart? Has it been a long time since someone thought you were worth the effort?

Someone does think you're worth the effort. The same One who put rings around Saturn wants to wrap a ring of love around you and keep you close for all eternity. His name is Jesus. Let your heart delight in knowing he is pursuing you.

My Scripture of Hope

If I rise on the wings of the dawn, if I settle on the far side of the sea, even there your hand will guide me, your right hand will hold me fast.

PSALM 139:9–10 NIV

My Hope to Hold On to and My Worries to Release

God's Promise of Hope to Me

There is nowhere I can go where God's love will not find me.

My Prayer

DAY 6

God Chose You

Before I made you in your mother's womb, I chose you.
JEREMIAH 1:5

You are heaven's custom design. God "formed you in your mother's body" (Isaiah 44:2). He designed your every detail.

At a moment before moments existed, the sovereign Creator resolved, "I will make ________" (your name goes in the blank). Then he continued with, "And I will make him/her ________ and ________ and ________ and ________" (fill those blanks with your characteristics—insightful, clever, detail oriented, restless).

Because you are God's idea, you are a good idea. What God said about Jeremiah, he said about you: "Before I made you in your mother's womb, I chose you. Before you were born, I set you apart for a special work" (Jeremiah 1:5).

What work? That question trips up a lot of well-meaning folks. God wouldn't let me do what I like to do—would he? Actually, he would. Your Designer couples the "want to" with the "able to." Your Father created you for a purpose. And he is too gracious to assign you to a life of misery.

What have you always done well? What have you always loved to do? Those desires and abilities aren't happenstance. Your "want tos" and "able tos" are gifts from your Creator. They intersect at a place called "divine." Our days are less hard when we are living out the gifts God has given us.

My Scripture of Hope

God is working in you to help you want to do and be able to do what pleases him.

PHILIPPIANS 2:13

My Hope to Hold On to and My Worries to Release

God's Promise of Hope to Me

I am God's custom design. He will enable me to live out the purpose he has assigned me—a purpose that will please him and bring joy to me.

My Prayer

DAY 7

God Has Made a Way

He leads me in the paths of righteousness.

Psalm 23:3 NKJV

It was, at once, history's most beautiful and most horrible moment. Jesus stood in the tribunal of heaven. Sweeping a hand over all creation, he pleaded, "Punish me for their mistakes. See the murderer? Give me his penalty. The adulteress? I'll take her shame. The bigot, the liar, the thief? Do to me what you would do to them. Treat me as you would a sinner."

And God did. "For Christ . . . suffered once for sins, the righteous for the unrighteous, to bring you to God" (1 Peter 3:18 NIV). God made a way for you to get to him.

The path of righteousness is a narrow, winding trail up a steep hill. At the top of the hill is a cross. At the base of the cross are bags. Countless bags full of innumerable sins. Calvary is the compost pile for guilt. Would you like to leave yours there as well?

Righteous. It's what God is. It's what we are not. And yes, it's what God requires us to be.

God could have taken one look at our definitely *not* righteous state, shaken the dust off his feet, and turned away. But he didn't. So when you feel unworthy, when you're carrying bags of innumerable sins, when the awareness of your own unrighteousness hits hard and causes you to doubt, question, and even fear, don't. *Don't.* Because God doesn't turn away.

My Scripture of Hope

God makes people right with himself through their faith in Jesus Christ.

ROMANS 3:22

My Hope to Hold On to and My Worries to Release

God's Promise of Hope to Me

God sent Jesus so I can be with him. When I put my faith in Jesus, he makes me right with God, and I can leave my sins and guilt at the cross.

My Prayer

DAY 8

Claim His Promise

I will not believe it until I see the nail marks in his hands and . . . put my hand into his side.

John 20:25

In our world of budgets, long-range planning, and computers, don't we find it hard to trust in the unbelievable? Don't most of us tend to scrutinize life with furrowed brows and walk with cautious steps? It's hard for us to imagine that God can surprise us. To make a little room for miracles today, well, it's not sound thinking.

We make the same mistake Thomas made, doubting that Jesus was alive after his crucifixion: We forget that *impossible* is one of God's favorite words.

How about you? How is your imagination these days? When was the last time you let your dream elbow out your logic? When was the last time you imagined the unimaginable? Has it been a while since you claimed God's promise to do "more than anything we can ask or imagine" (Ephesians 3:20)?

Think about all that God has promised you: Forgiveness for all your sins—past, present, and future. His own Holy Spirit to live inside you. A room prepared just for you. An eternity forever free of darkness, sadness, and tears—and every moment spent with him. Let these holy promises feed your hope when things seem impossible.

My Scripture of Hope

What he says he will do, he does. What he promises, he makes come true.

Numbers 23:19

My Hope to Hold On to and My Worries to Release

God's Promise of Hope to Me

God is able to do the impossible. He keeps every promise he makes.

My Prayer

DAY 9

Expectations

He is the One who loves us, who made us free
from our sins with the blood of his death.
REVELATION 1:5

When we love with expectations, we say, "I love you, but I'll love you even more if . . ." Christ's love has none of this. No strings, no expectations, no hidden agendas, no secrets. His love for us was, and is, up front and clear. "I love you," he says. "Even if you let me down. I love you in spite of your failures."

One step behind the expectations of Christ come his forgiveness and tenderness. Tumble off the tightrope of what our Master expects, and you land safely in his net of love.

Expectations. Alone, they can drag us to despair; but buffered by acceptance and forgiveness, they can bring out the best in us.

Does Christ demand a lot? You'd better believe it. Does he want much? Only our best. Does he have expectations? Just that we leave everything, deny all, and follow him. So what makes his expectations different from the world's? Forgiveness and acceptance. Jesus didn't demand perfection before coming to save you.

If expectations—from your boss, your spouse, yourself—overwhelm you, take refuge in the One whose expectations come with mercy and grace.

My Scripture of Hope

God's mercy is great, and he loved us very much. Though we were spiritually dead because of the things we did against God, he gave us new life with Christ. You have been saved by God's grace.

EPHESIANS 2:4–5

My Hope to Hold On to and My Worries to Release

God's Promise of Hope to Me

God's grace doesn't depend on me meeting a set of expectations. It depends on his perfect love.

My Prayer

DAY 10

God Is Near

All things were made by him, and nothing was made without him.

John 1:3

From where I write, I can see several miracles.

White-crested waves slap the beach with rhythmic regularity. One after the other, the rising swells of saltwater gain momentum, humping, rising, then standing to salute the beach before crashing onto the sand. How many billions of times has this simple mystery repeated itself since time began?

In the distance lies a miracle of colors—twins of blue. The ocean-blue of the Atlantic encounters the pale blue of the sky, separated only by the horizon.

Miracles. Divine miracles.

These are miracles because they are mysteries. Scientifically explainable? Yes. Reproducible? To a degree.

But still they are mysteries. Events that stretch beyond our understanding and find their origins in another realm. They are every bit as divine as divided seas, walking paralytics, and empty tombs.

And they declare that not only is God here, but he is near.

Could your life use a miracle? Are you waiting for someone to walk on water or to break open your chains?

The fact is, God is pouring his miracles into this world and into your life, minute by minute and moment by moment. Why? So you'll look up from the phone, the task list, the trouble and see that there's more to this life than the struggles of this world. So you'll see that he *is* God and that he *is* here with you. Look up!

My Scripture of Hope

The heavens declare the glory of God; the skies proclaim the work of his hands.

PSALM 19:1 NIV

My Hope to Hold On to and My Worries to Release

God's Promise of Hope to Me

The miracles of God are all around me. They declare that he is real and very, very near.

My Prayer

DAY 11

Perfect Grace

I will forgive their iniquity, and their sin I will remember no more.

JEREMIAH 31:34 NKJV

To love conditionally is against God's nature. Just as it's against your nature to eat trees and against mine to grow wings, it's against God's nature to remember forgiven sins.

You see, God is either the God of perfect grace . . . or he is not God. Grace forgets. Period. He who is perfect love cannot hold grudges. If he does, then he isn't perfect love. And if he isn't perfect love, you might as well put this book down and go fishing because both of us are chasing fairy tales.

But I believe in his loving forgetfulness. And I believe he has a graciously terrible memory.

So do yourself a favor. Leave your sins at the cross. Give them to God and let them go.

And don't forget to remember . . . he forgot.

Grace forgets, but do you? Is there something from your past that you can't seem to let go? Some secret, some shame, some sin that just seems too big to simply forget? Take it to God. Lay it at his feet and leave it there. Then remember God's perfect grace and this promise that he has made you new.

My Scripture of Hope

If anyone belongs to Christ, there is a new creation. The old things have gone; everything is made new!

2 CORINTHIANS 5:17

My Hope to Hold On to and My Worries to Release

God's Promise of Hope to Me

I can let go of my past. It is gone. Christ has made me new!

My Prayer

DAY 12

God's Story

How great is your goodness that you have stored up for those who fear you, that you have given to those who trust you.

Psalm 31:19

In heaven's finest act of love, God became human. Jesus Christ entered our jungle of hurt and heartache. He spoke with a voice we could trust and issued a message we dare not resist: *I've come to take you out of here.*

Not only did he talk to us; he died for us. It was necessary that he do so. Remember, God's garden is perfect. Yet God's children are anything but. When Jesus died on the cross, he died our death, paid our price, and took our place. He, the sinless, became a sinner so that we, the sinners, could be regarded as sinless.

God's dream has not changed. Consider his invitation: "Look! I have been standing at the door, and I am constantly knocking. If anyone hears me calling him and opens the door, I will come in and fellowship with him and he with me" (Revelation 3:20 TLB).

God's storyline concludes with you, me, and all his children living, ruling, dining, and serving with him in a perfect world.

> This world is a tangled mess of a story. But it's not the whole story, and it's definitely not the end of the story. Christ is the hero, and he is coming to rescue you, to deliver you. When life here gets hard, remember where this story is headed.

My Scripture of Hope

No one has ever seen this, and no one has ever heard about it. No one has ever imagined what God has prepared for those who love him.

1 Corinthians 2:9

My Hope to Hold On to and My Worries to Release

God's Promise of Hope to Me

God has prepared a place for me *with him*. It will be more wonderful than anything I could ever imagine.

My Prayer

DAY 13

What You Have

Rejoice in the Lord always. Again I will say, rejoice!
PHILIPPIANS 4:4 NKJV

How's life?" someone asks. And we who've been resurrected from the dead say, "Well, things could be better." Or, "I couldn't find a parking place." Or, "My parents won't let me move to Hawaii." Or, "People won't leave me alone so I can finish my sermon on selfishness."

Are you so focused on what you don't have that you are blind to what you do have?

You have a ticket to heaven that no thief can take, an eternal home that no divorce can break. Every sin of your life has been cast into the sea. Every mistake you've made was nailed to the tree.

You're blood bought and heaven made.

A child of God—forever saved.

So be grateful, joyful—for isn't it true? What you don't have is much less than what you do.

It's so easy to get caught up in "I wish I had" or "Why don't I have?" You don't mean to be selfish; it's just that your eyes are a bit too filled up with self and the stuff of the world and not enough of God. It happens to us all, which is why we all need an occasional wake-up call. It's why we all need to remember just how much we have.

My Scripture of Hope

Surely your goodness and love will follow me all the days of my life, and I will dwell in the house of the Lord forever.

Psalm 23:6 NIV

My Hope to Hold On to and My Worries to Release

God's Promise of Hope to Me

God's love and goodness are with me always. He invites me into his house to live with him forever.

My Prayer

DAY 14

You Can Trust Him

I will cause food to fall like rain from the sky for all of you. Every day the people must go out and gather what they need for that day.

EXODUS 16:4

God liberated his children from slavery and created a path through the sea. He gave them a cloud to follow in the day and a fire to see at night. And he gave them food. He met their most basic need: He filled their bellies.

Each morning, the manna came. Just as God promised. Each evening, the quail appeared. Just as God promised. He promised to meet their needs, one day at a time. But despite God's faithfulness in keeping his promise, the people had a hard time seeing food and not hoarding it.

"What if he forgets tomorrow? What if he doesn't come back?" So they would take more than one day's share of food. Overnight the food would spoil.

"Just take enough for today," was God's message. "Let me worry about tomorrow."

Do you worry about tomorrow? About where the next paycheck, the next meal, the next measure of patience will come from? God knows your worries.

Maybe you wonder why God doesn't simply remove the problem. Why he doesn't make the provision last. Why he doesn't supply tomorrow's needs today. The answer is that God wants to be more than your superstore. He wants to be the one you trust.

My Scripture of Hope

My God will use his wonderful riches in Christ Jesus to give you everything you need.

PHILIPPIANS 4:19

My Hope to Hold On to and My Worries to Release

God's Promise of Hope to Me

God knows what I need, and I can trust him to meet all my needs.

My Prayer

DAY 15

Know Where You're Headed

No one knows when that day or time will be, not the angels in heaven, not even the Son. Only the Father knows.

MATTHEW 24:36

"Where are you headed?"

There you have it. With one question, you are hereby equipped for travel chitchat. I use it often.

I've heard hundreds of answers. "Toledo." "Rio." "Tokyo." "Kokomo." But I've never, ever heard this reply: "I don't know."

Travelers know their destination, right? Travel 101 instructs, "Know where you're going." Wouldn't Life 101 say the same?

We are all headed somewhere. Each day brings us closer to a final breath, a final heartbeat, a final sigh. Shouldn't our destination be an obsession? The Bible certainly suggests as much. The New Testament mentions the return of Jesus more than three hundred times! And on some fifty occasions we are told to be ready.[1]

If quantity equates to priority, then life after this life is a crucial issue to God.

Canvass the Scripture's teachings about the future, and two themes repeatedly surface: It's all about hope, and it's all about him.

> You may not know the day or the time when Jesus will return. And you may not know exactly, down to the last detail, what his return will look like. But there is one thing you can know: your final destination. Because if you are a child of God, he has promised to return for you, to take you where he is.

My Scripture of Hope

After I go and prepare a place for you, I will come back and take you to be with me so that you may be where I am.

John 14:3

My Hope to Hold On to and My Worries to Release

God's Promise of Hope to Me

Jesus will come back for me. He will rescue me and take me to be with him for eternity.

My Prayer

DAY 16

What Do You Need?

LORD, I call to you. Come quickly. Listen to me when I call to you.

PSALM 141:1

Nicodemus came to Jesus in the middle of the night. The centurion came in the middle of the day. The leper and the sinful woman appeared in the middle of crowds. Zacchaeus appeared in the middle of a tree. Matthew had a party for him.

The educated. The powerful. The rejected. The sick. The lonely. The wealthy. Who would ever have assembled such a crew? All they had in common were their empty hope chests, long left vacant by charlatans and profiteers. And though they had nothing to offer, they asked for everything: a new birth, a second chance, a fresh start, a clean conscience. Yet without exception their requests were honored.

What do you need from Jesus? Not the earthly, superficial stuff but rather the eternal stuff. Chances are that your list looks a lot like those long-ago believers': to be reborn, have another chance, a new beginning, a clean conscience. Jesus honored their requests for such things, and you can trust that he will honor yours too.

My Scripture of Hope

If you remain in me and my words remain in you, ask whatever you wish, and it will be done for you.

John 15:7 NIV

My Hope to Hold On to and My Worries to Release

God's Promise of Hope to Me

God walks with me. He listens to my prayers, and he answers them . . . *perfectly*.

My Prayer

DAY 17

God's Love Won't Fail You

As high as the sky is above the earth, so great
is his love for those who respect him.

Psalm 103:11

The big news of the Bible is not that you love God but that God loves you; not that you can know God but that God already knows you! He tattooed your name on the palm of his hand. His thoughts of you outnumber the grains of sand on the shore. You never leave his mind, escape his sight, flee his thoughts.

He sees the worst of you and loves you still. Your sins of tomorrow and failings of the future will not surprise him; he sees them now. Every day and deed of your life has passed before his eyes and been calculated in his decision. He knows you better than *you* know you and has reached his verdict: He loves you still.

No discovery will disillusion him; no rebellion will dissuade him. He loves you with an everlasting love.

People may fail you. Jobs and friends may fail you. But God won't. His love is never failing and never ending. Nothing—not one thing—can make him love you any less. You cannot lose his love.

What do you do with a love like that? You rest in it. Sink back and soak in it. Let it seep deep inside, and then let it spill out into the world around you. Don't worry; you won't run out—because God's love is everlasting and immeasurable.

My Scripture of Hope

Neither death nor life, neither angels nor demons, neither the present nor the future, nor any powers, neither height nor depth, nor anything else in all creation, will be able to separate us from the love of God that is in Christ Jesus our Lord.

Romans 8:38–39 NIV

My Hope to Hold On to and My Worries to Release

God's Promise of Hope to Me

God's love for me cannot be measured. I can't lose it, and I don't have to earn it. It is mine simply because I am his.

My Prayer

Your Destiny

You have made them to be a kingdom and priests to serve our God, and they will reign on the earth.

REVELATION 5:10 NIV

You will reign with Christ. Pause and let that promise sink in. There is so much banter these days about self-image and identity. For want of a good self-image, we drive fast cars, liposuction fat, join gangs, or wear tight (or baggy) jeans.

Yet what better cure is there for a rotten self-image than the discovery of our eternal destiny! You aren't on a dead-end street. Your worth is not measured by the number of bucks in the bank or diplomas on your wall or followers on your socials or gadgets in your garage or tattoos on your skin.

What God did for Adam, he did for you. He formed you. He breathed life into you. And he destined you to serve him in a perfect place. Can you hear him? "I see something great in you. Would you accept my destiny for your life?"

Oh, I do pray you will.

The world can be cruel. Its judgments and ever-changing requirements can leave us feeling inadequate, marginalized, and sidelined. Society makes a big deal out of the rich and beautiful. Many of us are neither. Yet all feelings of insignificance will melt the moment Jesus, King Jesus, crowns and commissions us. Hold tight to that knowledge that our hope for hard days starts and ends with the reality that we are destined to serve and reign with our Savior.

My Scripture of Hope

> Just as my Father has given me a kingdom, I also give you a kingdom so you may eat and drink at my table in my kingdom.
>
> LUKE 22:29–30

My Hope to Hold On to and My Worries to Release

God's Promise of Hope to Me

Jesus has a place for me, not just in his kingdom but at his table. My true self and my destiny are found in him.

My Prayer

DAY 19

A Friendship Like No Other

All things are worth nothing compared with the greatness of knowing Christ Jesus my Lord.

PHILIPPIANS 3:8

The reward of Christianity is Christ.

Do you journey to the Grand Canyon for the souvenir T-shirt or the snow globe with the snowflakes that swirl when you shake it? No. The reward of the Grand Canyon is the Grand Canyon. The wide-eyed realization that you are part of something ancient, splendid, powerful, and greater than you.

The cache of Christianity is Christ. Not money in the bank or a car in the garage or a healthy body or a better self-image. Those are secondary and tertiary fruits perhaps. But the Fort Knox of faith is Christ. Fellowshipping with him. Walking with him. Pondering him. Exploring him. The heart-stopping realization that in him you are part of something ancient, endless, unstoppable, and unfathomable. And that he who can dig the Grand Canyon with his pinkie thinks you're worth his death on Roman timber. Christ is the reward of Christianity. And he's inviting you into a friendship like no other.

What are your motives for following Jesus? Are you simply trying to find your way through life, fit in at church, or avoid a fiery hereafter? Jesus is offering you so much more. He's inviting you into a relationship—a friendship like no other. With the *Son of God*.

If your faith is feeling stale or even faltering, take a look at your heart and remember who he wants to be for you.

My Scripture of Hope

I no longer call you servants, because a servant does not know what his master is doing. But I call you friends, because I have made known to you everything I heard from my Father.

JOHN 15:15

My Hope to Hold On to and My Worries to Release

God's Promise of Hope to Me

Jesus calls *me* his friend.

My Prayer

DAY 20

Would You Like to See Jesus?

If I go up to the heavens, you are there; if I make my bed in the depths, you are there.

PSALM 139:8 NIV

It is the normality, not the uniqueness, of God's miracles that causes them to be so staggering. Rather than shocking the globe with an occasional demonstration of deity, God has opted to display his power daily. Proverbially. Pounding waves. Prism-cast colors. Birth, death, life. We are surrounded by miracles. God is throwing testimonies at us like fireworks, each one declaring, "God is! God is!"

The psalmist marveled at such holy handiwork. "Where can I go from your Spirit?" he questioned with delight. "Where can I flee from your presence? If I go up to the heavens, you are there; if I make my bed in the depths, you are there" (Psalm 139:7–8 NIV).

With so many miraculous testimonies all around us, how could we escape God? But somehow we do.

Would you like to see Jesus? Do you dare be an eyewitness of his Majesty? Then rediscover amazement.

Next time you hear a baby laugh or see an ocean wave, take note. Pause and listen as his Majesty whispers, "I'm here."

Has the frequency of God's miracles blinded you to their beauty? Has the extraordinary become ordinary? Step out of your ho-hummery and into the presence and power of God. Rediscover your amazement. Be a child again. Be delighted. Be awed. There is no one like our God.

My Scripture of Hope

He performs wonders that cannot be fathomed, miracles that cannot be counted.

Job 5:9 NIV

My Hope to Hold On to and My Worries to Release

God's Promise of Hope to Me

The miracles of God cannot be counted. He is constantly at work in this world.

My Prayer

DAY 21

Your Covenant with God

God is not a human being, and he will not lie. He is not a human, and he does not change his mind.

NUMBERS 23:19 NCV

God's covenants serve like the autopilot feature on an airplane. Some years ago, I decided to pursue a pilot's license. My wife, Denalyn, groaned at the thought. I take wrong turns driving a car. What would I do in an airplane?

I tried to assuage her fears by describing the most amazing technology—the autopilot. Set the destination, and the plane stays on course.

Turns out, I never had the opportunity to use that technology. Life got complicated, and I had to quit the lessons. But the effort wasn't a total waste. I found a wonderful way to illustrate God's covenants. He has set history on autopilot. We are on a divine trajectory governed by his promises. What God has set out to do, he will do.

Our God is a covenant-making and covenant-keeping God. He does not lie. He *cannot* lie. His "royal decrees cannot be changed" (Psalm 93:5 TLB). God can no more break a promise than you and I can swim the Pacific Ocean.

God is not like us. We remake our decisions and reconsider our opinions. We are prone to break the promises we make at the tiniest unforeseen circumstance. But God doesn't. He sees the end of history. His decrees are not his *desire* for the future. They are his *description* of the future.

My Scripture of Hope

I am God . . . telling you what the ending will be—assuring you, "I'm in this for the long haul, I'll do exactly what I set out to do."

Isaiah 46:9–10 MSG

My Hope to Hold On to and My Worries to Release

God's Promise of Hope to Me

Only God is God. He will always do what he says he will do. I can trust the ending to him.

My Prayer

DAY 22

Lift Your Eyes

Do not let your hearts be troubled. You believe in God; believe also in me.

JOHN 14:1 NIV

On the eve of his crucifixion, Jesus told his followers what was going to happen the next day. He would be abandoned by his friends and killed by his enemies.

What news could be worse for them? Questions rose in their minds like waves on a stormy sea.

"How can this be?"

"What does he mean?"

"Where will we go?"

Yet before they could voice their fears, Jesus calmed them.

"Do not let your hearts be troubled. You believe in God; believe also in me. My Father's house has many rooms; if that were not so, would I have told you that I am going there to prepare a place for you?" (John 14:1–2 NIV).

Note what Jesus did. He lifted their eyes; he shifted their thoughts. In essence he said, "Think less about your present fears. Think much about your eternal home."

What would Jesus say to you today? Are your thoughts fixed on present fears or your eternal home? When your thoughts need to be nudged upward and onto him, remember that he makes our faith perfect.

My Scripture of Hope

Let us look only to Jesus, the One who began our faith and who makes it perfect.

HEBREWS 12:2 NCV

My Hope to Hold On to and My Worries to Release

God's Promise of Hope to Me

I will look to Jesus. He created my faith, and he will continue working to perfect it.

My Prayer

DAY 23

The God You Need

The LORD created the heavens. He is the God who formed the earth and made it.

ISAIAH 45:18 NCV

You don't need what Dorothy found. Remember her discovery in *The Wonderful Wizard of Oz*? She and her trio followed the Yellow Brick Road only to discover that the wizard was a wimp! Nothing but smoke and mirrors and tin-drum thunder. Is that the kind of god you want or seek?

You don't need to carry the burden of a lesser god . . . a god on a shelf, a god in a box, or a god in a bottle. No, you need a God who can place 100 billion stars in our galaxy and 100 billion galaxies in the universe. You need a God who can shape two fists of flesh into 75 to 100 billion nerve cells, each with as many as 10,000 connections to other nerve cells, place it in a skull, and call it a brain.

And you need a God who, while so mind-numbingly mighty, can come in the soft of night and touch you with the tenderness of an April snow.

You need a God. And you have one.

Dorothy's wannabe wizard hid behind a curtain and pretended to be a god when he was not. But the true God—Yahweh—took the curtain that separated his people from him and ripped it in two (Matthew 27:51). He doesn't hide from you; he invites you into his presence. He is powerful enough to take care of your every need and personal enough to know what those needs are.

My Scripture of Hope

Cast your cares on the LORD and he will sustain you; he will never let the righteous be shaken.

PSALM 55:22 NIV

My Hope to Hold On to and My Worries to Release

God's Promise of Hope to Me

God invites me to turn my troubles over to him. I can trust him. He will not let me down.

My Prayer

DAY 24

Eternal Instants

You have done good things for your servant,
as you have promised, Lord.
Psalm 119:65

Eternal instants. You've had them. We all have.

Sharing a porch swing on a summer evening with your grandchild.

Seeing your loved one's face in the glow of a candle.

Putting your arm through your spouse's as you stroll through the golden leaves and breathe the brisk autumn air.

Listening to your six-year-old thank God for everything from goldfish to Grandma.

Such moments are necessary because they remind us that everything is okay. The King is still on the throne, and life is still worth living. Eternal instants remind us that love is still the greatest possession, and the future is nothing to fear.

The next time an instant in your life begins to be eternal, let it.

Do you rush through your eternal instants? Do you tap your toes, waiting to get to the next thing?

Why the rush and hurry away from what matters most? Why the hurry to return to the ordinary? The next time you encounter an eternal instant—a priceless moment—resist the urge to cut it short. Don't interrupt the silence or shatter the solemnity. Soak it in. You're on holy ground.

My Scripture of Hope

God said, "Kneel and pray. You are in a holy place, on holy ground."

Acts 7:33 MSG

My Hope to Hold On to and My Worries to Release

God's Promise of Hope to Me

God puts eternal instants—priceless moments—into my life. And he invites me to stand with him there on holy ground.

My Prayer

DAY 25

Authored by God

I will praise You, for I am fearfully and wonderfully made.

PSALM 139:14 NKJV

How would you answer this multiple-choice question? "I am (A) a coincidental collision of particles; (B) an accidental evolution of molecules; (C) soulless flotsam in the universe, or (D) 'fearfully and wonderfully made.'"

Don't dull your life by missing this point: You are more than statistical chance, more than a marriage of heredity and society, more than a confluence of inherited chromosomes and childhood trauma. Thanks to God, you have been "sculpted from nothing into something" (Psalm 139:15 MSG).

Just as an artist takes a canvas into a studio, so God took you into his hidden chamber, where you were "woven together." The Master Weaver selected your temperament threads, your character texture, the yarn of your personality—all before you were born. God did not drop you into the world utterly defenseless and empty-handed. You arrived fully equipped.

You may not feel fully equipped or wonderfully made today. You might be facing something quite hard—but you are *you* for a God-designed reason. Does knowing that God himself designed you impact the way you think about yourself or your situation? Perhaps this is a day to give yourself some grace . . . and to accept his.

My Scripture of Hope

God created human beings in his image. In the image of God he created them. He created them male and female.

GENESIS 1:27

My Hope to Hold On to and My Worries to Release

God's Promise of Hope to Me

I am no accident. I was fearfully and wonderfully made by God, in the image of God.

My Prayer

DAY 26

Such a Savior

Sing to Him, sing psalms to Him; talk of all His wondrous works!
PSALM 105:2 NKJV

God has never taken his eyes off you. Not for a millisecond. He's always near. He lives to hear your heartbeat. He loves to hear your prayers. He loves you so much, he would rather die *for* your sin than let you die *in* your sin—so that's what he did.

What do you do with such a Savior? Don't you sing to him? Don't you declare, confess, and proclaim his name? Don't you bow a knee, lower a head, hammer a nail, feed the poor, and lift up your gift in worship? Of course you do.

Worship God. Applaud him loudly and often.

For your sake, because you need it.

And for heaven's sake, because he deserves it.

"God has never taken his eyes off you." It's not a condemnation; it's adoration . . . and it's an invitation. To rest in his love. To cease striving and stressing and worrying that you're not enough. To simply trust that you are loved.

No, God never takes his eyes off you, but can you say the same? Have the worries of this world pulled your eyes away from him? Want to fill your eyes with him again? The answer is simple: Praise him for his love and for his goodness. And praise him while you wait to see it in your life.

My Scripture of Hope

I remain confident of this: I will see the goodness of the Lord in the land of the living. Wait for the Lord; be strong and take heart and wait for the Lord.

Psalm 27:13–14 NIV

My Hope to Hold On to and My Worries to Release

God's Promise of Hope to Me

God's love for me is sure and certain. I can rest in it even as I wait to see his goodness at work in my life.

My Prayer

DAY 27

Show Up, Play Hard, Be Happy

Fight the good fight of faith, grabbing hold of the life that continues forever.
1 Timothy 6:12

Some years ago I attended a San Antonio Spurs basketball game, and it was unique because it did not matter. The Spurs had already won their division. They had already clinched the top seed in the playoffs. They could not lose, even if they lost.

The game was of little or no interest to the sports world. But it intrigued this preacher. I saw a sermon illustration waiting to happen. Christians occupy the same spot that the Spurs did. According to the Bible, we've already won. Our victory is secure. No one can snatch us from our Father's hand.

Yet we still have a few contests before the final conquest. So how do we behave in the meantime?

The Spurs were a good example. I've never seen a team enjoy a game more than they did that night. They were relaxed, confident, and happy. Because of that, they won the game.

That's our strategy. In these last days, show up, play hard, and be happy. After all, the victory is secure.

> As a child of God, your seat at the table in God's kingdom is already secured. But how are you living out your "until then"? Are you relaxed and confident? Are you showing up and playing hard? Are you happy? If you're struggling to stay in the game, remember—your team has already won the championship.

My Scripture of Hope

If what you heard from the beginning lives deeply in you, you will live deeply in both Son and Father. This is exactly what Christ promised: eternal life, real life!

1 John 2:25 MSG

My Hope to Hold On to and My Worries to Release

God's Promise of Hope to Me

Christ has promised me life—an eternal life with him. He always keeps his promises.

My Prayer

DAY 28

When You're Feeling Lost

We had to celebrate and be happy because your brother . . . was lost, but now he is found.

LUKE 15:32

When our oldest daughter, Jenna, was two, I lost her in a department store. One minute she was at my side, and the next she was gone. I panicked. All of a sudden only one thing mattered—I had to find my daughter. Shopping was forgotten. The list of things I came to get was unimportant. I yelled her name. What people thought didn't matter. For a few minutes, every ounce of energy had one goal—to find my lost child. (I did, by the way. She was hiding behind some jackets!)

No price is too high for a parent to pay to redeem his child. No energy is too great. No effort too demanding. A parent will go to any length to find their own. So will God.

God's greatest creation is not the flung stars or the gorged canyons. It's his eternal plan to reach his children. Heaven and earth know no greater passion than God's personal passion for you.

Have you ever wandered away and then looked up to realize you were lost? It's lonely and frightening, isn't it?

God will not leave you lost and wandering. He will search until he finds you. And when he does, it's not to scold you. It's to gather you up and hold you close to his heart. When you feel lost, remember that you are his beloved.

My Scripture of Hope

He tends his flock like a shepherd: He gathers the lambs in his arms and carries them close to his heart.

Isaiah 40:11 NIV

My Hope to Hold On to and My Worries to Release

God's Promise of Hope to Me

God will not leave me lost and wandering. He will search until he finds me. He will hold me close to his heart.

My Prayer

DAY 29

God Gives Hope

God will help you overflow with hope in him
through the Holy Spirit's power within you.
ROMANS 15:13 TLB

Heaven's hope does for your world what the sunlight did for my grandmother's cellar. It was a deep hole with wooden steps, plywood walls, and a musty smell. As a youngster I used to climb in, close the door, and see how long I could last in the darkness. I would sit silently, listening to my breath and heartbeats, until I couldn't take it anymore and would race up the stairs and throw open the door. Light would avalanche into the cellar. What a change!

Moments before, I couldn't see anything—and then suddenly, I could see everything.

Just as light poured into the cellar, God's hope pours into your world. Upon the sick, he shines the ray of healing. To the bereaved, he gives the promise of reunion. To the confused, he offers the light of Scripture.

God gives us the light of hope.

Are there days that feel like a dark cellar with the door tightly shut? Could you use a little—or an avalanche—of the light of God's hope? One day, all the wonder, peace, and perfection of heaven that you hope for will be reality. Until then, look for the light God is streaming into your life.

My Scripture of Hope

When Jesus spoke again to the people, he said, "I am the light of the world. Whoever follows me will never walk in darkness, but will have the light of life."

JOHN 8:12 NIV

My Hope to Hold On to and My Worries to Release

God's Promise of Hope to Me

Jesus is the light of the world. When I follow him, he lights up my path and chases away the darkness. He is my light, all my life.

My Prayer

DAY 30

The Master Plan

It was the L*ORD's will to crush him.*

ISAIAH 53:10 NIV

The cross was no accident.

Jesus' death was not the result of a panicking cosmological engineer. The cross wasn't a tragic surprise. Calvary was not a knee-jerk response to a world plummeting toward destruction. It wasn't a patch job or a stopgap measure. The death of the Son of God was anything but an unexpected peril.

No, it was part of a plan. It was a calculated choice. "It was the Lord's will to crush him" (Isaiah 53:10 NIV). The cross was drawn into the original blueprint. It was written into the script.

The moment the forbidden fruit touched Eve's lips, the shadow of a cross appeared on the horizon. And between that moment and the moment the man with the mallet placed the spike against the wrist of God, a master plan was fulfilled.

The cross wasn't a last-second, last-ditch decision. It was at the center of creation before creation began. Because God knew all along we would need it. Because God knew all along *you* would need it.

The cross was God's good and perfect plan to save the ones he loves . . . to save you. The next time you're wondering if the grace of the cross includes you, remember why Jesus came.

My Scripture of Hope

For God so loved the world that he gave his one and only Son, that whoever believes in him shall not perish but have eternal life.

John 3:16 NIV

My Hope to Hold On to and My Worries to Release

God's Promise of Hope to Me

God sent his Son because he loves me. Jesus gave up his life because he loves me. Because of the cross, I can live in that love forever.

My Prayer

DAY 31

Making the Impossible Possible

The things impossible for people are possible for God.

LUKE 18:27

God always rejoices when we dare to dream. In fact, we are much like God when we dream. The Master exults in newness. He delights in stretching the old. He wrote the book on making the impossible possible.

Examples? Check the Book.

Eighty-year-old shepherds don't usually play chicken with Pharaohs . . . but don't tell that to Moses.

Teenage shepherds don't normally have showdowns with giants . . . but don't tell that to David.

Night-shift shepherds don't usually get to hear angels sing and see God in a stable . . . but don't tell that to the Bethlehem bunch.

And for sure don't tell that to God. He's made an eternity out of making the earthbound airborne. And he gets angry when people's wings are clipped.

Has someone clipped your wings? Might it even have been you? Is it doubt or fear that keeps your feet firmly planted in the nest? Or perhaps it's the uncertainties that spring up like wildfires in this unpredictable world that keep you from testing out your wings.

If you need the impossible to happen in your life, don't declare it to be . . . well, impossible. Turn it over to God, and see what he has to say about it.

My Scripture of Hope

Oh, Lord God, you made the skies and the earth with your very great power. There is nothing too hard for you to do.

Jeremiah 32:17

My Hope to Hold On to and My Worries to Release

God's Promise of Hope to Me

God can do anything. And he has promised to do good things for me.

My Prayer

DAY 32

Your Strong Father

Look to the Lord *and his strength; seek his face always.*

1 Chronicles 16:11 NIV

When my daughters were toddlers, we had a sophisticated bedtime routine. The girls knew how to extend our good night time so they wouldn't have to go to sleep. "Be funny, Daddy," they'd say. And I would comply. I'd bump my nose on the door or trip and fall on the floor. They'd laugh and then say, "Be goofy, Daddy." I'd comply with a clown face and silly expressions. They'd laugh again, but they wouldn't let me leave without responding to one final request. "Be strong, Daddy."

I'd flex my muscles. I'd stand tall like a grizzly and chase all the shadows away.

I like to think that the sight of a strong daddy helped them settle down and sleep.

It certainly helps us, right?

We have a strong Father. Strong enough to make a million galaxies yet near enough to chase away every shadow of the night.

Keep looking to him.

> Do you need a father who is strong? One who will flex his muscles and chase away all your shadows? Shadows of self-doubt and fear. Shadows of struggle and trouble. Shadows of just being so tired of having to get up and do it all over again and again. That's exactly the kind of Father you have. Look to him and remember—he *is* light.

My Scripture of Hope

LORD, you give light to my lamp. My God brightens the darkness around me.

PSALM 18:28

My Hope to Hold On to and My Worries to Release

God's Promise of Hope to Me

God shines his light into my life. He is my strong Father who chases away the shadows and the darkness.

My Prayer

DAY 33

Assurance of Victory

This is the victory that conquers the world—our faith.

1 JOHN 5:4

What is unique about the kingdom of God is that you are assured of victory. You have won! You are assured that you will someday stand before the face of God and see the King of kings. You are assured that someday you will enter a world where there will be no more pain, no more tears, no more sorrow.

If you have no faith in the future, then you have no power in the present. If you have no faith in the life beyond this life, then your present life is going to be powerless. But if you believe in the future and are assured of victory, then there should be a dance in your step and a smile on your face.

You've won! Not just once or twice. Not just for a lifetime. You've won for an eternity. That's the promise God gives you when you choose to believe in him. So when the days hit hard and you feel like you're losing, hold tight to your hope and remember this: Victory is already yours!

My Scripture of Hope

In all these things we are completely victorious through God who showed his love for us.

ROMANS 8:37

My Hope to Hold On to and My Worries to Release

God's Promise of Hope to Me

No matter what happens in this world, I have victory in Jesus. I have already won the best possible reward . . . for eternity.

My Prayer

DAY 34

In His Hands

When he, the Spirit of truth, comes, he will guide you into all the truth. He will not speak on his own; he will speak only what he hears, and he will tell you what is yet to come.

John 16:13 NIV

No person can claim to have an airtight forecast of the future. Only God knows the details of tomorrow. However, we can claim this promise: "[The Holy Spirit] will tell you what is yet to come" (John 16:13 NIV). God spent a great deal of time and ink telling us what to expect. It honors him and does the soul good to ponder his plans.

In the book of Revelation, God is identified as "Almighty" eight different times.[1] The Greek term is *pantokrator*—a compound of two Greek words: *panto* (everything) and *kratein* (to hold). God holds everything! At the helm of history is a God who not only rules the age but controls the calendar. We can speculate about the order of events, but we need never wonder about the certainty of the outcome. He holds the world in his hands.

You can't know the future. None of us can. And there are details of God's plan that remain a mystery to everyone but God the Father. So while you may not know all the whens, wheres, and hows, you can know the heart of the God who has them all perfectly planned. He's spelled it out in his Word and spilled it out on a rough Roman cross. If your questions ever make you question, remember that God's plan for you is good.

My Scripture of Hope

"I know the plans I have for you," declares the Lord, "plans to prosper you and not to harm you, plans to give you hope and a future."

Jeremiah 29:11 NIV

My Hope to Hold On to and My Worries to Release

God's Promise of Hope to Me

I can know God's heart even when I don't know his plans. And his heart is filled with love and good plans for me.

My Prayer

DAY 35

A Personal Invitation

Come to me . . . and I will give you rest.

Matthew 11:28

When Jesus says, "Come to me," he doesn't say to come to religion, come to a system, or come to a certain doctrine. This is a very personal invitation to a God, an invitation to a Savior.

Our God is not aloof—he's not so far above us that he can't see and understand our problems. Jesus isn't a God who stayed on the mountaintop—he's a Savior who came down and lived and worked among the people. Everywhere he went, crowds followed, drawn together by the magnet that was—and is—the Savior.

The life of Jesus Christ is a message of hope, a message of mercy, a message of life in a dark world. It's a message for all people. And it's a message he personally extends to you.

> So much of this world can feel impersonal, uncaring, cold. How often are you just another number, another face, another rat in the race? But that's what makes the personal invitation of God even more amazing. Because, yes, God invites everyone. But every invitation is personal. He knows your name, your heart, and the number of hairs on your head—and he invites you to know and follow him. Remember, with God, it's always personal.

My Scripture of Hope

My sheep listen to my voice; I know them, and they follow me.

JOHN 10:27 NIV

My Hope to Hold On to and My Worries to Release

God's Promise of Hope to Me

Jesus knows me *personally*. He invites me—*personally*—to follow him.

My Prayer

DAY 36

Death Isn't the End

Your life is like a mist. You can see it for a short time, but then it goes away.

James 4:14

You, as with all God's children, live one final breath from your own funeral.

Which, from God's perspective, is nothing to grieve. He responds to these grave facts with this great news: "The day you die is better than the day you are born" (Ecclesiastes 7:1 NLT).

Now, there is a twist. Heaven enjoys a maternity-ward reaction to funerals. Angels watch body burials the same way grandparents monitor delivery-room doors: "He'll be coming through any minute!" They can't wait to see the new arrival. While we're driving hearses and wearing black, they're hanging streamers and celebrating. We don't grieve when babies enter the world. The hosts of heaven don't weep when we leave it.

The angels don't weep at the thought of death, but do you? Do you dread death? And is that dread robbing you of the joy of life? Is it keeping you from fully stepping into the life you were created to live? Because that's why Jesus came. To free you from death's sting. Death isn't an ending; it's the turn of a page and a step into a glorious new chapter.

When fear and dread creep into your heart, don't let them rob you of today's joy, of today's adventures. Instead, remember why Jesus did what he did.

My Scripture of Hope

Since these children are people with physical bodies, Jesus himself became like them. He did this so that, by dying, he could destroy the one who has the power of death—the devil.

HEBREWS 2:14–15

My Hope to Hold On to and My Worries to Release

God's Promise of Hope to Me

Death has no power over me. Jesus has taken away its sting. I don't have to worry about what comes next because Jesus is already there waiting for me.

My Prayer

Jesus Will Come!

Jesus, who has been taken up from you into heaven, will come in the same way as you have watched Him go into heaven.

ACTS 1:11 NASB

Jesus will come! Not "may come" or "might come." Jesus *will* come! His promised return is not a nebulous, vapid, cross-your-fingers aspiration. It is a concrete, guaranteed appearance of our Savior.

Jesus validated his return by vacating his tomb. This was the conviction of the apostle Paul: "The truth is that Christ *has* been raised up, the first in a long legacy of those who are going to leave the cemeteries" (1 Corinthians 15:20 MSG).

Is the tomb of Jesus empty? Did he defang death? Did Christ discard his shroud like a bad habit and march out of the tomb?

The resounding answer is "Yes." His tomb floor has the prints of pierced feet. Those feet were nailed to a cross on Friday and lifeless in the grave on Saturday. But on Sunday the hope of Easter called them to stand, step up, and walk out of the grave. When Jesus vacated the tomb, he populated the heart of humanity with hope.

There are a lot of unknowns in this world. But there is one thing you can know without a shadow of a doubt: *Jesus will return.* The *how, when*, and *where* are a mystery, but the *why* is not. Because God loves you. He knew right from the start that you were going to need hope in this hard world. So he sent his Son.

My Scripture of Hope

In God's great mercy he has caused us to be born again into a living hope, because Jesus Christ rose from the dead.

1 Peter 1:3 NCV

My Hope to Hold On to and My Worries to Release

God's Promise of Hope to Me

God is merciful and good. Because Jesus rose again, I have the hope—the promise—of eternity with him.

My Prayer

DAY 38

Simply Because You Are You

I'll call the unloved and make them beloved.

ROMANS 9:25 MSG

Our love depends on the receiver of the love. Let a thousand people pass before us, and we will not feel the same about each. Our love will be regulated by their appearance, by their personality. Even when we find a few people we like, our feelings will fluctuate. How they treat us will affect how we love them. The receiver regulates our love.

Not so with the love of God. We have no thermostatic impact on his love for us. The love of God is born from within him, not from what he finds in us. His love is uncaused and spontaneous.

Does he love us because of our goodness? Because of our kindness? Because of our great faith? No, he loves us because of *his* goodness, kindness, and great faith.

What do you do to be loved? What decisions do you make? What risks do you take? How vulnerable do you have to make yourself to be loved by those in your world?

Want to know what you have to do to be loved by God? Nothing. His love is yours. Period. A gift to hold on to, rely on, and keep forever. Simply because you are you and he is God.

My Scripture of Hope

We know and rely on the love God has for us. God is love. Whoever lives in love lives in God, and God in them.

1 John 4:16 NIV

My Hope to Hold On to and My Worries to Release

God's Promise of Hope to Me

God loves me. I can count on his love. He will not stop loving me.

My Prayer

DAY 39

Keep Your Eyes on the Cross

Christ . . . suffered once for sins, the righteous for the unrighteous, to bring you to God.

1 Peter 3:18 NIV

One of the reference points of London is the Charing Cross. It is near the geographical center of the city and serves as a navigational tool for those confused by the streets.

One day, a little girl was lost in the great city. A police officer found her. Between sobs and tears, she explained she didn't know her way home. He asked her if she knew her address. She didn't. He asked her phone number; she didn't know that either. But when he asked her what she did know, suddenly her face lit up.

"I know the cross," she said. "Show me the cross and I can find my way home from there."

So can you. Keep a clear vision of the cross on your horizon, and you can find your way home.

How do you keep a clear vision of the cross? When the office is hectic, the kids are chaotic, and the weekend has become more about catching up than slowing down, how do you keep your eyes on Jesus?

Of all the commands God gave us, this might be one of the toughest: Slow down.

Don't let the wonder of the cross whiz by in a blur of busyness. Pause for a day of rest—to relax your body and restore your vision. Get your bearings so you can find your way home. And when life feels too busy to allow for rest, turn to Jesus, the source of true rest.

My Scripture of Hope

Truly my soul finds rest in God; my salvation comes from him.

Psalm 62:1 NIV

My Hope to Hold On to and My Worries to Release

God's Promise of Hope to Me

I can rest in God. He is my salvation.

My Prayer

DAY 40

Everything You Need

The Lord is my shepherd; I have everything I need.

Psalm 23:1

May I meddle for a moment? What is the one thing separating you from joy? How do you fill in this blank: "I will be happy when _________"? *When I am healed. When I am promoted. When I am married. When I am single. When I am rich.* How would you finish that statement?

Now, with your answer firmly in mind, answer this: If your ship never comes in, if your dream never comes true, if the situation never changes, could you be happy? If not, then you need to know what you have in your Shepherd.

You have a God who hears you, the power of love behind you, the Holy Spirit within you, and all of heaven ahead of you. If you have the Shepherd, you have grace for every sin, direction for every turn, a candle for every corner, and an anchor for every storm. You have everything you need.

What's your "I'll be happy when _________" statement? When you hold that statement up to the riches of God's grace and the promise of heaven, does it change?

Surrender all your "I'll be happy whens" to the Shepherd who's promised to give you everything you need. Then you'll discover what he gives you in exchange: peace, contentment, and sorrow-resistant gratitude.

My Scripture of Hope

Be content with what you have, because God has said, "Never will I leave you; never will I forsake you."

HEBREWS 13:5 NIV

My Hope to Hold On to and My Worries to Release

God's Promise of Hope to Me

My God, my Shepherd, watches over me. He will never leave or abandon me. I can be content because he is all I truly need.

My Prayer

DAY 41

He's Been There

He had to enter into every detail of human life.

HEBREWS 2:17 MSG

You've barely dipped a toe into Matthew's Gospel when you realize that Jesus hails from the Tilted Halo Society. In his bloodline, we find that Rahab was a Jericho harlot. Grandpa Jacob was slippery enough to warrant an electric ankle bracelet. David had a personality as irregular as a Picasso painting—one day writing psalms, another day seducing his soldier's wife. But did Jesus erase their names from the list? Not at all.

Why did Jesus hang his family's dirty laundry on the neighborhood clothesline?

Because your family has some too. The dad who never came home. The grandparent who ran away with the coworker. If your family tree has bruised fruit, then Jesus wants you to know, "I've been there."

The phrase "I've been there" is in the chorus of Christ's theme song. To the lonely, Jesus whispers, "I've been there." To the discouraged, Christ nods his head and sighs, "I've been there."

Family is a tricky thing, isn't it? Sometimes wonderful. Sometimes . . . *not.* Earthly families can create a refuge like no other and a turmoil like no other. When you're hurting and in need of a reminder of the perfect family to come, remember this: You are a child of God, and he calls you by name.

My Scripture of Hope

Now you . . . are not foreigners or strangers any longer, but are citizens together with God's holy people. You belong to God's family.

EPHESIANS 2:19

My Hope to Hold On to and My Worries to Release

God's Promise of Hope to Me

Because I believe, I am a citizen of God's kingdom. I belong to God's family.

My Prayer

DAY 42

Run to Jesus!

His love has taken over our lives; GOD's faithful ways are eternal.

PSALM 117:2 MSG

God's love for you is not dependent on how you look, how you think, how you act, or how perfect you are. His love is absolutely nonnegotiable and nonreturnable. Ours is a faithful God.

No matter what you do, no matter how far you fall, no matter how ugly you become, God has a relentless, undying, unfathomable, unquenchable love from which you cannot be separated. Ever!

Run to Jesus. Jesus wants you to go to him. He wants to become the most important person in your life, the greatest love you'll ever know. He wants you to love him so much that there's no room in your heart or in your life for sin. Invite him to take up residence in your heart. He will.

> So much of your life is conditional, isn't it? Conditional on looking, thinking, and acting a certain way. Conditional on doing and saying the right things. Conditional . . . and uncertain. But Christ's love for you is not conditional. It's sure and certain. A rock to stand on. Just like his ability to save you. When you believe in him, nothing can take his love away.

My Scripture of Hope

I give them eternal life, and they shall never perish; no one will snatch them out of my hand.

JOHN 10:28 NIV

My Hope to Hold On to and My Worries to Release

God's Promise of Hope to Me

I am saved by God's mercy and grace. No one can snatch me away from him.

My Prayer

DAY 43

Yes, You're Included

For God so loved the world that He gave His only begotten Son.
JOHN 3:16 NKJV

As boldly as the center beam of the cross proclaims God's holiness, the crossbeam declares his love. And oh, how wide his love reaches.

Aren't you glad the verse doesn't read, "For God so loved the rich"? Or, "For God so loved the famous"? Or, "For God so loved the thin"?

It doesn't. Nor does it state, "For God so loved the Europeans or the Africans," "the sober or the successful," or "the young or the old."

No, when we read John 3:16, we simply (and happily) read, "For God so loved the world."

How wide is God's love? Wide enough for the whole world.

Are you included in the world? Then you are included in God's love.

You aren't always included, are you? Universities exclude you if you aren't smart enough. Businesses exclude you if you aren't qualified enough, and sadly, some churches even exclude you if you aren't "good" enough.

But not Jesus. You're included in his love. Always. And if you begin to doubt, question, or even to wonder about his love for you, just remember what he chose to do for you.

My Scripture of Hope

Christ carried our sins in his body on the cross so we would stop living for sin and start living for what is right. And you are healed because of his wounds.

1 Peter 2:24

My Hope to Hold On to and My Worries to Release

God's Promise of Hope to Me

Christ died to save me from sin and give me a new life with him. His wounds have healed me.

My Prayer

DAY 44

Don't Give Up!

It is finished.

John 19:30

Our inability to finish what we start is seen in the smallest of things—a partly mowed lawn, a half-read book. Sometimes it shows up in life's most painful areas—an abandoned child, a wrecked marriage.

Any chance I'm addressing someone who is considering giving up? If I am, I want to encourage you to remain. I want to encourage you to remember Jesus' determination on the cross.

Jesus didn't quit. But don't think for one minute that he wasn't tempted to. Did he ever want to quit? You bet.

That's why his words are so splendid. "It is finished."

Are you close to quitting? Discouraged? Even weary of doing good? Is *hope* a forgotten word? Remember, a finisher is not the one with no wounds or weariness (think of Jesus on that cross).

When life's challenges tempt you to throw in the towel, hold on. Please don't quit. Give it one more shot. Remain, endure, and remember this promise: He's not just *with* you; he is *in* you.

My Scripture of Hope

Remain in me, and I will remain in you. A branch cannot produce fruit alone but must remain in the vine. In the same way, you cannot produce fruit alone but must remain in me.

John 15:4

My Hope to Hold On to and My Worries to Release

God's Promise of Hope to Me

When I remain in Jesus, he remains in me. He will help me not only endure but thrive.

My Prayer

DAY 45

Love Covers Everything

He saves my life from the grave and loads me with love and mercy.

Psalm 103:4

It's time to let God's love cover all things in your life. All the secrets. All the hurts. All the hours of evil. All the minutes of worry.

The years you peddled prejudice and pride? His love will cover that. The mornings you awoke in the bed of a stranger? His love will cover that. Every promise broken, drug taken, penny stolen. Every cross word, cussword, and harsh word. His love covers all things.

Let it. Discover along with the psalmist: "He . . . loads me with love and mercy."

Picture a giant dump truck full of love. There you are behind it. God lifts the bed until the love starts to slide. Slowly at first, then down, down, down until you are hidden, buried, covered in his love.

"Hey, where are you?" someone asks.

"In here," you reply, "covered in love."

Does that kind of love seem impossible? After all, you know how far from perfection you've fallen. If someone did to you the things you've done to God—turned away from him, denied him with words and actions both big and small—you'd find it all but impossible to forgive, wouldn't you? But not God.

When you find yourself searching for hope and struggling to trust the vastness of God's love for you, remember that he specializes in the impossible and the unimaginable.

My Scripture of Hope

God can do anything, you know—far more than you could ever imagine or guess or request in your wildest dreams!

Ephesians 3:20 MSG

My Hope to Hold On to and My Worries to Release

God's Promise of Hope to Me

God can do anything. He can—and will—forgive my every mistake, blunder, and sin. Why? Because he loves me more than I could ever imagine.

My Prayer

DAY 46

God Will Praise You

God will praise each one of them.

1 Corinthians 4:5

What an incredible promise. "God will praise each one of them." Not "the best of them" or "a few of them" or "the achievers among them."

God will praise *each one* of them.

God does not delegate the job. The angel Michael doesn't hand out the crowns. Moses doesn't speak on behalf of the throne. God himself does the honors.

That day is coming. God will put a crown on your head and a hand on your shoulder and bless you.

Each child you hugged, he will praise you for it. Every time you forgave, he will praise you for it. Every penny you offered, truth you taught, prayer you prayed—he will praise you for it. He'll praise you for the day you refused to give in and the season you refused to give up. But most of all, he'll praise you for saying yes to Jesus.

Remember the best praise you've ever received. It felt good, didn't it? If you're like me, you'd probably like some more. Yet doesn't it sometimes seem like so much of the good you do goes without notice, without praise, without even a thanks? It can be discouraging.

If you grow weary of doing good that no one seems to see or praise, remember that God does. He sees and praises and does not forget.

My Scripture of Hope

God . . . will not forget the work you did and the love you showed for him by helping his people.

HEBREWS 6:10

My Hope to Hold On to and My Worries to Release

God's Promise of Hope to Me

God sees my efforts. He doesn't forget the good I try to do. And one day, He will praise me for it. *Personally.*

My Prayer

DAY 47

Who God Sees

As many of you as were baptized into Christ have put on Christ.

GALATIANS 3:27 RSV

You read it right. We have "put on" Christ. When God looks at us, he doesn't see us; he sees Christ. We "wear" him. We are hidden in him; we are covered by him. As the song says, "Dressed in his righteousness alone, faultless to stand before the throne."[1]

Presumptuous, you say? Sacrilegious? It would be if it were my idea. But it isn't; it's his. We are presumptuous, not when we marvel at his grace but when we reject it. And we're sacrilegious not when we claim his forgiveness but when we allow the haunting sins of yesterday to convince us that God forgives but he doesn't forget.

Do yourself a favor. Remember . . . he forgot.

Who do you see in the mirror? Or maybe I should ask, *What* do you see in the mirror? Mistakes you struggle to forget? The person you were instead of the person you wish you had been? Maybe now is a good time to remind yourself of who and what God sees when he looks at you.

My Scripture of Hope

I delight greatly in the LORD; my soul rejoices in my God. For he has clothed me with garments of salvation and arrayed me in a robe of his righteousness.

ISAIAH 61:10 NIV

My Hope to Hold On to and My Worries to Release

God's Promise of Hope to Me

God sees Christ in me. Therefore I am clothed in his spotless robe of righteousness.

My Prayer

DAY 48

What Can You Do for the King?

At the name of Jesus every knee should bow, in heaven and on earth and under the earth.

PHILIPPIANS 2:10 NIV

Knowing that we shall kneel before Jesus one day, how should we live today? An example of readiness is seen in Arlington National Cemetery. The men and women who guard the Tomb of the Unknown Soldier display a level of unparalleled fidelity. They devote eight hours to the preparation of their uniforms. Gloves are worn wet to improve the grip on the rifle.

The sentinel repeats the same walk over and over: twenty-one steps, then shift the rifle to the other shoulder, then twenty-one more steps. The routine never varies, not even at night, when the cemetery is closed. When Hurricane Isabel moved through the area in 2003, the soldiers never stopped. Trees fell and the wind whipped, but they kept their post. Remarkable.

Question: If they can display such allegiance rightly given to unknown, dead soldiers, can we not do the same for our living, coming, ruling King?

> What can you do today in honor of your King? What kindness can you perform? What offense can you forgive? What temptation can you resist? What gift can you offer? What discipline can you begin? What sacrifice can you make? What act of love can you show? Remember, whatever you do, do it for him.

My Scripture of Hope

I tell you the truth, anything you did for even the least of my people here, you also did for me.

MATTHEW 25:40

My Hope to Hold On to and My Worries to Release

God's Promise of Hope to Me

When I serve others, I serve Jesus. He will see and bless me.

My Prayer

DAY 49

No Accident

I lay down my life for the sheep.

John 10:15 NIV

Our Master lived a three-dimensional life. He had as clear a view of the future as he did of the present and the past.

This is why the ropes the soldiers used to tie his hands and to lead him to the cross were unnecessary. They were incidental. Had they not been there, had there been no trial, no Pilate and no crowd, the very same crucifixion would have occurred. Had Jesus been forced to nail himself to the cross, he would have done it. For it was not the soldiers who killed him nor the screams of the mob. It was his devotion to us.

So call it what you wish: an act of grace, a plan of redemption, a martyr's sacrifice. But whatever you call it, don't call it an accident. It was anything but that.

Accident. Coincidence. Happenstance. Why do we work so hard to brush away the wonder of God's grace? Why do we pretend his sacrifice wasn't personal or planned? When you need a reminder that his gift of grace was no accident, remember Isaiah's prophecy revealing God's plan.

My Scripture of Hope

He poured out his life unto death, and was numbered with the transgressors. For he bore the sin of many, and made intercession for the transgressors.

Isaiah 53:12 NIV

My Hope to Hold On to and My Worries to Release

God's Promise of Hope to Me

Jesus knows me, and I can know him. He will shepherd me through this life and into forever with him.

My Prayer

DAY 50

Living on Tiptoe

At that time people will see the Son of Man coming in clouds with great power and glory.

MARK 13:26 NIV

Peter spent most of his later years living in Jerusalem. How many times did he take the brief walk to the Mount of Olives and reflect on the words of the angel—"He will come back." Did he search the clouds? Contemplate the heavens? Reflect on the angel's promise? "Jesus . . . will come in the same way as you have watched Him go" (Acts 1:11 NASB).

Three decades later, that's what he urged his readers to do: "Set your hope completely on the grace to be brought to you at the revelation of Jesus Christ" (1 Peter 1:13 NASB).

The Christian lives life on tiptoe, ever searching the skies. We awaken with the thought, *Perhaps today!* Our hope is centered on the bodily return of Christ. We are looking to a new age in which Jesus will be crowned as the rightful King and we will serve as his grateful servants. All of history is headed to the great day that will inaugurate an endless era of justice, joy, and glory.

Are you living on tiptoe, ever searching the skies? Or are your feet firmly stuck in the muck and mire of this world? Just know that you were created for so much more than that. God's hand is ever ready to lift you out and help you stand on the solid rock he's prepared for you.

My Scripture of Hope

He lifted me out of the slimy pit, out of the mud and mire;
he set my feet on a rock and gave me a firm place to stand.

Psalm 40:2 niv

My Hope to Hold On to and My Worries to Release

God's Promise of Hope to Me

God will lift me up above the struggles of this world. He will give me a firm place to stand while I watch and wait for Jesus' return.

My Prayer

DAY 51

Listen for God's Music

The Lord disciplines those he loves.

HEBREWS 12:6

Oh, how God wants you to hear his music.

He has a rhythm that will race your heart and lyrics that will stir your tears. You want to journey to the stars? He can take you there.

You want to lie down in peace? His music can soothe your soul.

But first, he's got to get rid of that country-western stuff. (Forgive me, Nashville. Only an example.)

And so he begins deleting the playlists. A friend turns away. The job goes bad. Your spouse doesn't understand. The church is dull. One by one, he removes the options until all you have left is God.

Would he do that? Absolutely. If he must silence every voice, he will. He wants you to hear his music.

Don't wait for God to silence all those other voices. Turn down the volume yourself. Step away. Get away with God. Turn off the phones, the alerts, the screens. Simply be still and listen for his music. Know that he alone is God (Psalm 46:10) and you are his.

My Scripture of Hope

Know that the Lord is God. It is he who made us, and we are his.

Psalm 100:3 NIV

My Hope to Hold On to and My Worries to Release

God's Promise of Hope to Me

God is Lord over all. He made me, and I am his; he disciplines me out of love.

My Prayer

DAY 52

Jesus Did It for You

All things are worth nothing compared with the greatness of knowing Christ Jesus my Lord.

PHILIPPIANS 3:8

Want to know the coolest thing about Christ's coming?

Not that the One who hung the galaxies gave it up to hang doorjambs to the displeasure of a cranky client who wanted everything yesterday but couldn't pay for anything until tomorrow.

Not that he refused to defend himself when blamed for every sin of every single human since Adam.

Not even that after three days in a dark hole, he stepped into the Easter sunrise with a smile and a swagger and a question for lowly Lucifer—"Is that your best punch?"

That was cool, incredibly cool.

But want to know the coolest thing about the One who gave up the crown of heaven for a crown of thorns?

He did it for you. Just for you.

The Son of God left heaven to be born in a lowly stable, to live as a man, to be mocked and ridiculed, to be spat upon, to be beaten and hung on a cross. Just trying to wrap your mind around those truths is almost impossible, isn't it? But the reason he did it? *He did it for you.* Let that sink deep into the broken places needing to be mended. And then praise him for this truth.

My Scripture of Hope

Christ entered the Most Holy Place only once—and for all time. He did not take with him the blood of goats and calves. His sacrifice was his own blood, and by it he set us free from sin forever.

Hebrews 9:12

My Hope to Hold On to and My Worries to Release

God's Promise of Hope to Me

Christ sacrificed himself for me. *For me.* To set me free from my sins forever.

My Prayer

DAY 53

Not Hard to Love

The Lord *loves you.*

Deuteronomy 7:8 NLT

God loves you simply because he has chosen to do so. He loves you when you don't feel lovely. He loves you when no one else loves you.

Others may abandon you, divorce you, and ignore you, but God will love you. Always. No matter what.

This is his sentiment: "I'll call nobodies and make them somebodies; I'll call the unloved and make them beloved" (Romans 9:25 MSG).

This is his promise: "I have loved you, my people, with an everlasting love. With unfailing love I have drawn you to myself" (Jeremiah 31:3 NLT).

Do you know what else that means? You have a deep aquifer of love from which to draw. When you find it hard to love, then you need a drink.

Drink deeply! Drink daily!

Do you ever have a moment—or more—when you feel unlovely, even unlovable? You're not. Not to God.

God doesn't love you because of what you do or even how much you do for him. Your goodness doesn't increase his love, nor does your weakness diminish it. You are endlessly and perfectly loved simply because God has chosen to love you. So the next time you're feeling less than lovable, saturate your heart in this truth.

My Scripture of Hope

See what great love the Father has lavished on us, that we should be called children of God! And that is what we are!

1 John 3:1 NIV

My Hope to Hold On to and My Worries to Release

God's Promise of Hope to Me

God *lavishes* his love on me. He calls me his child. And that is who I am!

My Prayer

DAY 54

The Wedding

The kingdom of heaven is like a certain king who arranged a marriage for his son.

MATTHEW 22:2 NKJV

We all have favorite wedding moments: the candle lighting, the groom appearing, the rice tossing, the cake cutting. The selection is not easy to make.

It may surprise you, then, to learn that one moment is consistently chosen over any other. We love the arrival of the bride.

But not nearly as much as Jesus does.

Christ longs to see his bride. His Father has circled the date on the calendar of heaven. The groom is preparing a mansion. Heaven is abuzz with wedding fever. Scripture can't stop talking about the big event!

Why does Scripture describe the great day as a wedding day? The answer comes quickly, doesn't it? Something happens at a wedding that happens on no other day, in no other event. The intimacy, romance, physical union, complete surrender. Our union with Jesus is not one of master and slave or creator and created. It is husband and wife. Our arrival in heaven is understood not as a takeover, merger, or amalgamation but as a wedding between Christ and his bride, the church.

Plans are already underway for a heavenly wedding. The Bridegroom has taken care of all the details. There's nothing for you to worry over or try to fix. He's even given you the wedding clothes—pure and spotless and white as snow. Wrap yourself in them and remember.

My Scripture of Hope

[Jesus] died so that he could give the church to himself like a bride in all her beauty.

EPHESIANS 5:27

My Hope to Hold On to and My Worries to Release

God's Promise of Hope to Me

Jesus sacrificed himself so that I could come to the wedding pure, spotless, and without fault.

My Prayer

DAY 55

Before the World Began

When God put [Adam and Eve] in charge of everything,
nothing was excluded. But we don't see it yet, don't
see everything under human jurisdiction.
HEBREWS 2:8 MSG

At creation, humankind was charged with ruling the world. But we don't. Instead of ruling the world, we feel ruled *by* the world. We see creation in a state of corruption, eruption, and pollution.

What's more, rather than behaving as partners, people often act as rivals. Something is awry. What happened?

Sin happened. Rebellion happened. Satan happened. He convinced the couple that the garden, resplendent and abundant, was inadequate. Eden was not enough for Adam and Eve. They wanted to be like God. And God, who knows what is best for his creation, said, "No." He temporarily suspended the garden-of-Eden plan. But he did not cancel it or abandon it.

He certainly did not abandon us. Just the opposite.

God set in motion a plan of redemption that includes promises, prophets, miracles . . . and his own Son.

When sin entered the garden, God didn't throw his hands up and say, "Well, I didn't see that coming. What am I going to do now?" No. God already knew (and knows) the lousy choices we humans make. He has factored our selfishness, sinfulness, and, yes, even our stupidity into his plans and into his promise to save us.

My Scripture of Hope

In Christ, [God] chose us before the world was made so that we would be his holy people.

Ephesians 1:4

My Hope to Hold On to and My Worries to Release

God's Promise of Hope to Me

God chose me to be his child. Even before the world was made, he had a plan to rescue me.

My Prayer

Relentless Pursuit

When they heard the sound of God strolling in the garden in the evening breeze, the Man and his Wife hid in the trees of the garden, hid from God.

Genesis 3:8 msg

The overarching message of the Bible is God's relentless pursuit of his family. What he decreed in heaven is declared through creation. He will have his garden. He will share it with his children. Our names have been written into the grand narrative of God.

But what have we done in response? We have resisted the One who came to save us.

Adam and Eve did so. They hid from God! We've been hiding ever since. Adam and Eve covered themselves in fig leaves. We cover ourselves in works or status. They ducked into the trees. We hide in the foliage of denial, pride, or shame.

God, never easily put off, sought them out. He asked a question that has rung through the ages: "God called to the Man: 'Where are you?'" (Genesis 3:9 msg). This was not a question of geography. God knew their location. This was a question of the heart.

Step out of the shrubbery. Stop hiding. Let God find and rescue you.

Ever since Eve took that first bite of the forbidden fruit, God has been on a divine rescue mission. He's been sending out message after message, miracle after miracle, mercy after mercy to get our attention. Are you paying attention? Look, listen, believe, and remember.

My Scripture of Hope

Suppose one of you has a hundred sheep and loses one of them. Doesn't he leave the ninety-nine in the open country and go after the lost sheep until he finds it?

LUKE 15:4 NIV

My Hope to Hold On to and My Worries to Release

God's Promise of Hope to Me

God searches for those who are lost and wandering. He searches until he finds them. If I wander, God will search until he finds me.

My Prayer

DAY 57

It's Not Up to You

The Spirit speaks to God for his people in the way God wants.
ROMANS 8:27

None of us pray as much as we should, but all of us pray more than we think, because the Holy Spirit turns our sighs into petitions and our tears into entreaties. He speaks for you and protects you. He makes sure you get heard.

Now, suppose a person never learns about the sealing and intercession of the Spirit. This individual thinks that salvation security resides in oneself, not God, that prayer power depends on the person, not the Spirit. What kind of life will this person lead? A parched and prayerless one.

But what if you believe in the work of the Spirit? Will you be different as a result? You bet your sweet Sunday you will. Your shoulders will lift as you lower the buckling weight of self-salvation. Your knees will bend as you discover the buoyant power of the praying Spirit. Higher walk. Deeper prayers. And most of all, a quiet confidence that comes from knowing it's not up to you.

Jesus lived among us for thirty-three years. Don't you think he knew our faith would need some ongoing help? That *you* would need ongoing help? So Jesus did what he promised to do and gave you all you truly need (Philippians 4:19). Take heart and remember this gift to you.

My Scripture of Hope

I will ask the Father, and he will give you another Helper to be with you forever—the Spirit of truth.

John 14:16–17

My Hope to Hold On to and My Worries to Release

God's Promise of Hope to Me

It's not all up to me. The Holy Spirit is with me to help me . . . forever.

My Prayer

DAY 58

Everything God Wants You to Be

Each of us is an original.
Galatians 5:26 msg

God made you *you-nique.* Secular thinking, as a whole, doesn't buy this. Secular society sees no author behind the book, no architect behind the house, no purpose behind or beyond life. It simply says, "You can be anything you want to be."

Be a butcher if you want to, a sales rep if you like. Be an ambassador if you really care. You can be anything you want to be. But can you? If God didn't pack within you the meat sense of a butcher, the people skills of a salesperson, or the world vision of an ambassador, can you be one? An unhappy, dissatisfied one perhaps. But a fulfilled one? No.

You cannot be anything you want to be. But you can be everything God wants you to be. And when you do the most what you do the best, you put a smile on God's face. What could be better than that?

God never prefabs people. Only intentional—*and infinitely personal*—crafting and equipping. But the voices of this world will tell you that you're not one in a million; rather, you're one *of* a million.

When your situation seems empty of hope, ask yourself this: Are you listening to them or to him? Could it be that joy is waiting just on the other side of daring to be everything God created you to be? Remember who made you and how.

My Scripture of Hope

I praise you because I am fearfully and wonderfully made;
your works are wonderful, I know that full well.

Psalm 139:14 NIV

My Hope to Hold On to and My Worries to Release

God's Promise of Hope to Me

I am fearfully and wonderfully made *by God himself.* When I do what he created me to do, I make God smile.

My Prayer

DAY 59

Covered with Love

Love . . . always protects.

1 Corinthians 13:4–7 NIV

When Paul said, "Love always protects," he might have been thinking of a coat. One scholar thinks he was. The *Theological Dictionary of the New Testament* is known for its word study, not its poetry. But the scholar sounds poetic as he explains the meaning of *protect* as used in 1 Corinthians 13:7. The word conveys, he says, "the idea of covering with a cloak of love."

Remember receiving a cloak of love? You were nervous about the test, but the teacher stayed late to help you. You were far from home and afraid, but your mother phoned to comfort you. You were innocent and accused, so your friend stood to defend you. Covered with encouragement.

Covered with tenderhearted care. Covered with protection. *Covered with a cloak of love.*

Chances are you sang these words as a child: "Jesus loves me, this I know." But do you know? Do you know just how great his love for you is? Yes, great enough to die on a cross. But also great enough to show up every day in so many ways in your life. Read through the verses of 1 Corinthians 13:4–8. Drop God's name in the place of *love*, and know how completely covered you are in the cloak of his love.

My Scripture of Hope

[Love] always protects, always trusts, always hopes, always perseveres. Love never fails.

1 Corinthians 13:7–8 niv

My Hope to Hold On to and My Worries to Release

God's Promise of Hope to Me

I am loved by God. Perfectly and completely. His love will never fail me.

My Prayer

DAY 60

God Chose You

We love because God first loved us.

1 JOHN 4:19

When Beckham was a toddler, he was found wandering the streets of Burundi looking for food. An adoption alert went out and caught the attention of Maegan and Thomas. The couple already had two children and were praying for a third.

The law required the family to spend a week with Beckham to test compatibility. Happy to oblige, the family picked up the boy and drove to a beach house. The week was glorious. The days were filled with laughter, games, and joy.

On the last evening, Maegan and Thomas heard Beckham crying in his room. "Was I good enough?" he asked. He had been told the trip was a test. Only if he was good enough would he get a new home.

Thomas held Beckham close and assured him, "We chose you before we ever knew you. We made a promise, and we will keep it."

Our Father has made an identical promise to his children, and he will keep it.

God *chose* you to be his. Before you were born, before your first mistake, before your first rebellious sin, God *chose* you to be his. Even after all those mistakes and moments of rebellion—past, present, and still to come—he chooses you still.

My Scripture of Hope

Because of his love, God had already decided to make us his own children through Jesus Christ. That was what he wanted and what pleased him, and it brings praise to God because of his wonderful grace.

Ephesians 1:5–6

My Hope to Hold On to and My Worries to Release

God's Promise of Hope to Me

God chose me to be his child. It's what he wanted, and it pleases him.

My Prayer

DAY 61

An Ocean of Mercy

[God] has not punished us as our sins should be punished.

PSALM 103:10

Do you really think you haven't done things that hurt Christ? Have you ever been dishonest with his money? That's cheating. Ever gone to church to be seen rather than to see him? Hypocrite.

Ever broken a promise you've made to God? Don't you deserve to be punished? And yet, here you are. Reading this book. Breathing. Still witnessing sunsets and hearing babies gurgle. Still watching the seasons change. There are no lashes on your back or hooks in your nose or shackles on your feet. Apparently God hasn't kept a list of your wrongs.

Listen. You have not been sprinkled with forgiveness. You have not been spattered with grace. You have not been dusted with kindness. You have been immersed in it. You are submerged in mercy. You are a minnow in the ocean of his mercy. Let it change you!

Perfection. In so many areas of your life, that's what you're going for, isn't it? Perfection in your career, in your relationships, in your appearance. And honestly, how often do you attain it? Practically never. (Don't worry. It's a universal truth.) And certainly never in the area of faith. Which is one more reason to be grateful for the ocean of God's mercy you swim in. But be more than grateful . . . be changed by it.

And if you need a little more reassurance that perfection isn't what God is requiring, remember that Jesus came for us before we were changed.

My Scripture of Hope

God demonstrates his own love for us in this: While we were still sinners, Christ died for us.

Romans 5:8 NIV

My Hope to Hold On to and My Worries to Release

God's Promise of Hope to Me

I don't have to be perfect to be perfectly loved by God.

My Prayer

DAY 62

You Don't Have to Live with Your Sins

He was wounded for the wrong we did. . . . And we are healed because of his wounds.
Isaiah 53:5

In order for the cross of Christ to be the cross of our lives, we each need to bring something to the hill.

We have seen what Jesus brought. With scarred hands he offered forgiveness. Through torn skin he promised acceptance. He took the path to take us home. He wore our garment to give us his own. We have seen the gifts he brought.

Now we ask, What will we bring?

Why don't you start with your bad moments?

Those bad habits? Leave them at the cross. Your selfish moods and white lies? Give them to God. Your binges and bigotries? God wants them all. Every flop, every failure. He wants every single one. Why? Because he knows we can't live with them.

God doesn't want you to live with your mistakes. And while forgiveness is an unbelievably extraordinary gift, that's not all God wants to do. He wants to remove your sins too. Go ahead . . . leave them with him, along with your guilt and shame. He knows just what to do with them. And he promises to make us clean and pure and holy.

My Scripture of Hope

If we confess our sins, he will forgive our sins, because we can trust God to do what is right. He will cleanse us from all the wrongs we have done.

1 John 1:9

My Hope to Hold On to and My Worries to Release

God's Promise of Hope to Me

I can trust God to forgive my sins. He will make me clean again.

My Prayer

DAY 63

Only One Cure

He has filled them with skill.

Exodus 35:35 NIV

You were born prepacked. God looked at your entire life, determined your assignment, and gave you the tools to do the job.

Before traveling, you do something similar. You consider the demands of the journey and pack accordingly. Cold weather? Bring a jacket. Business meeting? Carry the laptop. Time with grandchildren? Better take some sneakers and pain medication.

God did the same with you. *Joe will research animals . . . install curiosity. Rachel will lead a private school . . . add an extra dose of management.*

I need Eric to comfort the sick . . . include a healthy share of compassion. Denalyn will marry Max . . . instill a double portion of patience.

God packed you on purpose for a purpose. Is this news to you? If so, you may be living out of the wrong bag. Isn't it time you found the bag God packed for you?

Imagine grabbing the wrong bag at the airport. Same size, material, and color as yours. But one peek inside, and the mistake is clear. Would you cram yourself into the wrong clothes? Of course not! You'd hunt down your bag. No one wants to live out of som one else's bag.

But are you? Has someone urged you into a life that doesn't quite fit? Then no wonder life is hard! There's only one cure: Ask God to lead you to the life he has packed for you.

My Scripture of Hope

We are God's handiwork, created in Christ Jesus to do good works, which God prepared in advance for us to do.

Ephesians 2:10 NIV

My Hope to Hold On to and My Worries to Release

God's Promise of Hope to Me

I was handcrafted by God. He has purpose for me and for my life.

My Prayer

DAY 64

You Don't Have to Be Afraid

The Father has loved us so much that we are called children of God.

1 JOHN 3:1

When my oldest daughter, Jenna, was four, she came to me with a confession: "Daddy, I took a crayon and drew on the wall." (Kids amaze me with their honesty.)

I sat down, lifted her into my lap, and tried to be wise. "Is that a good thing to do?" I asked her.

"No."

"What does Daddy do when you write on the wall?"

"You punish me."

"What do you think Daddy should do this time?"

"Love."

Don't we all want that? Don't we all long for a father who, even though our mistakes are written all over the wall, will love us anyway?

We do have that type of father. A father who is at his best when we are at our worst. A father whose grace is strongest when our devotion is weakest. A father who drenches us in his perfect love.

Whether your earthly father handled your mistakes with wisdom and grace, there is always a bit of fear when you've messed up. A fear of not being good enough to be loved.

You don't have to be afraid with your heavenly Father. Why? Because Jesus took your punishment upon himself, and he gifted you with grace. God's love for you is perfect, and perfect love drives out fear.

My Scripture of Hope

Where God's love is, there is no fear, because God's perfect love drives out fear.

1 John 4:18

My Hope to Hold On to and My Worries to Release

God's Promise of Hope to Me

God's love for me is perfect and complete. I have no reason to fear. I am safe inside God's love.

My Prayer

DAY 65

Jesus Understands

The One who comes from above is greater than all.

John 3:31

The idea that God would select a virgin to bear himself . . . The notion that God would don a scalp and toes and two eyes . . . The thought that the King of the universe would sneeze and burp and get bitten by mosquitoes . . . It's too incredible. Too revolutionary. We would never create such a Savior. We aren't that daring.

When we create a redeemer, we keep him safely distant in his faraway castle. We allow him only the briefest encounters with us. We permit him to swoop in and out with his sleigh before we can draw too near. We wouldn't ask him to take up residence among a contaminated people. In our wildest imaginings, we wouldn't conjure a king who becomes one of us.

But God did.

God became Immanuel—God with us. He suffered all that you've suffered just so he could understand. So that when hard times happen—and don't they always—he would understand and be able to help you. And so that he could say, "I've been where you've been, and I know just the right answer for you."

Jesus is the Savior you need who not only rescues and redeems but also understands.

My Scripture of Hope

Our high priest is able to understand our weaknesses. He was tempted in every way that we are, but he did not sin.

HEBREWS 4:15

My Hope to Hold On to and My Worries to Release

God's Promise of Hope to Me

Jesus understands my struggles. He's faced them all too. And he knows just how to help me.

My Prayer

DAY 66

Will You Choose God?

Let us come near to God with a sincere heart and a sure faith.

HEBREWS 10:22

It would have been nice if God had let us order life like we order a meal. I'll take good health and a high IQ. I'll pass on the music skills, but give me a fast metabolism . . . Would've been nice. But it didn't happen. When it came to your life on earth, you weren't given a voice or a vote.

But when it comes to life after death, you were. In my book, that seems like a good deal. Wouldn't you agree?

Have we been given any greater privilege than that of choice? Not only does this privilege offset any injustice; the gift of free will can offset any mistakes.

You've made some bad choices in life, haven't you? You've chosen the wrong friends, maybe the wrong career, even the wrong spouse. You look back over your life and say, "If only I could make up for those bad choices." You can. One good choice for eternity offsets a thousand bad ones on earth.

The choice is yours.

Long ago, Joshua declared, "As for me and my family, we will serve the LORD" (Joshua 24:15). Is that your choice too? No matter what the rest of the world—or perhaps even the rest of your family and friends—are doing, will you choose God? Will you believe in and follow his Son? It won't always be easy, but it's the only way to eternal life.

My Scripture of Hope

Jesus answered, "I am the way and the truth and the life. No one comes to the Father except through me."

JOHN 14:6 NIV

My Hope to Hold On to and My Worries to Release

God's Promise of Hope to Me

Jesus came to make a way for me to be with God. He is the only way to God. When I choose to follow him, he leads me to eternal life.

My Prayer

DAY 67

God Has Room for You

The angel who talked to me held in his hand a gold measuring stick to measure the city, its gates, and its wall. . . . Its length and width and height were each 1,400 miles.

REVELATION 21:15–16 NLT

Behold the size of the New Jerusalem: fourteen hundred miles in length, width, and height. Large enough to contain the land mass from the Appalachians to the West Coast and Canada to Mexico.

And that's just the ground floor. The city stands as tall as it is wide. Supposing God stacks the city in stories like a building, the New Jerusalem will have six hundred thousand floors. Ample space for billions of people.[1] Ample space for you.

When did you discover the congestion of this world? Your father's schedule had no space for you. Your boss just couldn't find a space for you. The school had no space for you.

We learn early the finite nature of resources. There's not much space. Consequently, we get eliminated, cut, dropped, and refused.

But with the dimensions of our soon-to-be home, God proclaims, "Enough space for all!"

Where have you been pushed out and told there is no room? Where have you been sidelined? A crowded lunch table, a members-only meeting, or perhaps a no-room-for-you church clique? That won't happen in God's new kingdom. Why? Jesus is there, not just saving a place but preparing a place just for you.

My Scripture of Hope

There are many rooms in my Father's house . . . I am going there to prepare a place for you.

John 14:2

My Hope to Hold On to and My Worries to Release

God's Promise of Hope to Me

There is room for me in God's house. Jesus is already there, preparing a place just for me.

My Prayer

Jesus Took Your Place

Christ . . . changed places with us and put himself under that curse.
GALATIANS 3:13

While on the cross, Jesus felt the indignity and disgrace of a criminal. No, he was not guilty. No, he had not committed a sin. And no, he did not deserve to be sentenced. But you and I were, we had, and we did. We were left with nothing to offer but a prayer.

And then, "he changed places with us." He wore our sin so we could wear his righteousness.

We come to the cross dressed in sin, but we leave the cross dressed in the "coat of his strong love" (Isaiah 59:17) and girded with a belt of "goodness and fairness" (1:5) and clothed in "garments of salvation" (61:10).

Indeed, we leave dressed in Christ himself. "You have all put on Christ as a garment" (Galatians 3:27 NEB).

Jesus willingly lifted your sin and shame from your shoulders on the way to the cross. As far as he is concerned, it's gone. Over. Finished. You don't have to carry it anymore. But are you? Are you still holding on to the tattered rags of guilt for your sins? Are you struggling to accept the spotless garment of righteousness Jesus is offering you?

Make the trade. Accept the exchange. Take the clothes Christ is offering you and be set free.

My Scripture of Hope

In Christ we are set free by the blood of his death, and so we have forgiveness of sins. How rich is God's grace, which he has given to us so fully and freely.

Ephesians 1:7–8

My Hope to Hold On to and My Worries to Release

God's Promise of Hope to Me

In Christ, I am fully forgiven and set free from my sins. I am covered and clothed in God's rich grace.

My Prayer

DAY 69

Your Invitation

All you who are thirsty, come and drink.

Isaiah 55:1

To receive an invitation is to be honored—to be held in high esteem. For that reason, all invitations deserve a kind and thoughtful response.

But the most incredible invitations are not found in envelopes or fortune cookies; they are found in the Bible. You can't read about God without finding him issuing invitations. He invited Eve to marry Adam, the animals to enter the ark, David to be king, Israel to leave bondage, Nehemiah to rebuild Jerusalem. God is an inviting God. He invited Mary to birth his Son, the disciples to fish for men, the adulterous woman to start over, and Thomas to touch Jesus' wounds. God is the King who prepares the palace, sets the table, and invites his subjects to come in.

God is a God who invites. A God who calls. A God who opens the door and waves his hand, pointing pilgrims to a full table. His invitation is not just for a meal; it is for life. An invitation to enter his kingdom. Forever.

There's something wonderful about being invited, isn't there? But do you ever wonder if the invitation is really for you?

Don't let the rejections of the past leave you wondering. Accept God's invitation and become his own.

My Scripture of Hope

To all who did accept him and believe in him he gave the right to become children of God.

JOHN 1:12

My Hope to Hold On to and My Worries to Release

God's Promise of Hope to Me

God's invitation is for me. And when I accept, I become his own child.

My Prayer

God with You

They shall call His name Immanuel, which is translated, "God with us."
MATTHEW 1:23 NKJV

God's treatment for insignificance won't lead you to a bar or dating service, a spouse or social club. God's ultimate cure for the common life takes you to a manger. The babe of Bethlehem. Immanuel. Remember the promise of the angel? "'Behold, the virgin shall be with child, and bear a Son, and they shall call His name Immanuel,' which is translated, 'God with us'" (Matthew 1:23 NKJV).

Immanuel. The name appears in the same Hebrew form as it did two thousand years ago. *Immanu* means "with us." *El* refers to *Elohim*, or God. He is not an "above us God" or a "somewhere in the neighborhood God." He came as the "with us God." *God with us.* Not "God with the rich" or "God with the religious," but God with us.

God with *you*.

Do you ever wrestle with loneliness? Feeling insignificant? Unnoticed and unknown? God's got a cure for that: His Son. Jesus not only knows and notices you, but you are so important to him that he came to earth to be *Immanuel* . . . for you.

The next time you're feeling hopeless and tempted to fill that emptiness with whatever the world has to offer, remember, God is with you.

My Scripture of Hope

A thief comes to steal and kill and destroy, but I came to give life—life in all its fullness.

JOHN 10:10

My Hope to Hold On to and My Worries to Release

God's Promise of Hope to Me

Jesus knows and notices me. He came to give me life in all its fullness!

My Prayer

DAY 71

What You Can't Do

Here is my servant whom I have chosen. I love him, and I am pleased with him.
MATTHEW 12:18

Those who saw Jesus—really saw him—knew there was something different. At his touch, beggars who were blind saw. At his command, crippled legs walked. At his embrace, empty lives filled with vision.

He fed thousands with one basket. He stilled a storm with one command. He raised the dead with one proclamation. He changed lives with one request. He rerouted the history of the world with one life, was born in one manger, and died on one hill . . . God did what we wouldn't dare dream.

He did what we couldn't imagine. He became a man so we could trust him. He became a sacrifice so we could know him. And he defeated death so we could follow him.

It defies logic. It is a divine insanity. A holy incredibility. Yet it is the very impossibility of it all that makes it possible.

Only a Creator beyond the fence of logic could offer such a gift of love.

What you can't do, God does.

So many things you can do, but the one thing that really matters—for eternity—is something you could never do for yourself. You can't save yourself. You can't study enough, work enough, or plan enough. And that's okay. Because God sent Jesus to make a way.

My Scripture of Hope

This is how God showed his love to us: . . He sent his Son to die in our place to take away our sins.

1 JOHN 4:9–10

My Hope to Hold On to and My Worries to Release

God's Promise of Hope to Me

God sent his Son to save me, to take away my sins, and to give me a new life in him. That is real love, and that is how God loves *me*.

My Prayer

One Day

Now I saw a new heaven and a new earth, for the first heaven and the first earth had passed away.

Revelation 21:1 NKJV

The pearl is born out of pain.

So it is with the New Jerusalem. It will be born out of the pain of Jesus. Throughout eternity, the pearly gates will remind us of our Savior, who took on the sin of the earth so we could experience the glory of heaven.

Speaking of our Savior, he will make the city splendid. But it won't be the golden streets, the emeralds, or structures that capture our hearts. It will be our Jesus. We will see him! We will touch the scarred hands, hear the calm voice. We will know him intimately. "The throne of God and of the Lamb will be in it, and His bond-servants will serve Him; they will see His face."

Pause and personalize that passage. Whisper to yourself (or shout it if you prefer), "I will see his face" (Revelation 22:2–4 NASB).

You will see God. You! You will see the One who has never not been, the One who has never given in, the One before whom all creation bows. You will see the God of all glory.

God told Moses, "You cannot see my face, because no one can see me and live" (Exodus 33:20). You will though. On the other side of eternity, you will see God face-to-face. It's impossible to imagine. But one day, this unimaginable moment you can't imagine will be your reality.

My Scripture of Hope

Now we see only a reflection as in a mirror; then we shall see face to face.

1 Corinthians 13:12 niv

My Hope to Hold On to and My Worries to Release

God's Promise of Hope to Me

One day, I will walk on streets of gold. I will live where there is no darkness. And I will look into the face of God.

My Prayer

DAY 73

You Belong to God

The love of God has been poured out in our hearts by the Holy Spirit.

Romans 5:5 NKJV

Deep within you, God's Spirit confirms with your spirit that you belong to him. Beneath the vitals of the heart, God's Spirit whispers, "You are mine. I bought you and sealed you, and no one can take you." The Spirit offers an inward, comforting witness.

He is like a father who walks hand in hand with his little child. The child knows he belongs to his daddy, his small hand happily lost in the large one. He feels no uncertainty about his papa's love. But suddenly the father, moved by some impulse, swings his boy up into the air and into his arms and says, "I love you, son."

Has the relationship between the two changed? On one level, no. The father is no more the father than he was before the expression of love. But on a deeper level, yes. The dad drenched, showered, and saturated the boy in love. God's Spirit does the same with us. The Holy Spirit pours the love of God in our hearts.

Take a look at Romans 5:5 again. Notice the preposition *of.* The Holy Spirit pours the love *of* God into your heart, not love *for* God (though you're gonna want that too). It's as if God hands a bucket of love to the Spirit and instructs, "Douse their heart." *You belong to the Father. Signed, sealed, and soon-to-be delivered.*

So when the challenges of this world make you question—make you fear—that maybe you don't really belong, listen to the voice of the Spirit inside.

My Scripture of Hope

The Spirit we received does not make us slaves again to fear; it makes us children of God.

ROMANS 8:15

My Hope to Hold On to and My Worries to Release

God's Promise of Hope to Me

I am God's child. I don't have to be afraid—I belong to him.

My Prayer

DAY 74

When the Rejections Come

He will rejoice over you with gladness, He will quiet you with His love.
ZEPHANIAH 3:17 NKJV

Suppose on your windowsill is a solitary daisy. This morning you picked the daisy and pinned it on your lapel.

But as soon as you're out the door, people start picking petals off your daisy. Someone snags your subway seat. Petal picked. You're blamed for a coworker's bad report. More petals. By the end of the day, you're down to one. You are one petal-snatching away from a blowup.

But now let's alter the scenario slightly. Let's add one character. The kind man in the apartment next door runs a flower shop. Every night on the way home, he stops at your place with a fresh bouquet. Because of him, your apartment has a sweet fragrance, and your step has a happy bounce. Let someone mess with your flower, and you've got a basketful to replace it!

God hand delivers a bouquet to your door every day. Open it! Take them! Then, when rejections come, you won't be left short-petaled.

Some days it feels like rejections are coming from every direction. That's what the evil one wants you to think. He might even whisper that one of those rejections is from God, that you've messed up one too many times, and God has crossed you off his list.

Don't believe it. God isn't crossing you off any list . . . he's too busy rejoicing that you are his.

My Scripture of Hope

The Lord delights in those who fear him, who put their hope in his unfailing love.

Psalm 147:11 NIV

My Hope to Hold On to and My Worries to Release

God's Promise of Hope to Me

God delights in me. His love will never fail me.

My Prayer

DAY 75

Imagine

He who sat on the throne said, "Behold, I make all things new."

Revelation 21:5 NKJV

Can you imagine God's kingdom?

I can't either. But what joy is found in the attempt.

When I was a youngster, my dad took the family to visit the Six Flags Over Texas theme park. I cannot overstate my excitement. The highlight of my two-stoplight hometown was an evening at Dairy Queen. Six Flags was everything our little town was not: colorful, musical, entertaining.

At one point while riding a trolley, I turned to my father and said, "This is the most wonderful place I have ever seen."

To which he responded, "That's great, Max. But we are still in the parking lot."

I had assumed the passenger shuttle was the big ride. I would have taken a tour of the entryway and called it a wonderful vacation. Good thing my father was there to tell me, "There's more on the other side."

That is God's message to you. He has a place for you, space for you, and grace for you. Lift your eyes and set your heart on your heavenly home. There is so much more on the other side.

The things of this world don't last. Thieves take, rust ruins, and moths munch away. But the things of God's kingdom? They last forever. You may live *in* this world, but don't be *of* it. Keep your eyes and your heart set on eternal things. And wait with joyful expectation for the promised day.

My Scripture of Hope

He will wipe every tear from their eyes, and there will be no more death or sorrow or crying or pain. All these things are gone forever.

Revelation 21:4 NLT

My Hope to Hold On to and My Worries to Release

God's Promise of Hope to Me

One day, everything will be better than I could ever imagine. No sorrow, death, or pain. Only joy and wonder and God. Forever.

My Prayer

DAY 76

Just a Moment

We shall all be changed—in a moment, in the twinkling of an eye.

1 CORINTHIANS 15:51–52 NKJV

I am with you always" are the words of a God who in one instant did the impossible to make it all possible for you and me (Matthew 28:20 NKJV).

It all happened in a moment. In one most remarkable moment. The Word became flesh.

There will be another. The world will see another instantaneous transformation. You see, in becoming man, God made it possible for man to see God. When Jesus went home, he left the back door open. As a result, "we shall all be changed—in a moment, in the twinkling of an eye."

The first moment of transformation went unnoticed by the world. But you can bet the second one won't. The next time you use the phrase "just a moment," remember that's all the time it will take to change the world.

Our lives can change in a moment. We know that, don't we? But those "momentary" changes here on this earth aren't always what we hope for. A day is coming, though, when the whole world will change in a moment, when Christ returns and calls us home. Until then, remember that he has promised you a place there too.

My Scripture of Hope

When you believed, you were marked in him with a seal, the promised Holy Spirit, who is a deposit guaranteeing our inheritance until the redemption of those who are God's possession—to the praise of his glory.

Ephesians 1:13–14 NIV

My Hope to Hold On to and My Worries to Release

God's Promise of Hope to Me

I am sealed by God with his Holy Spirit. I am guaranteed an inheritance in his kingdom.

My Prayer

DAY 77

An Invitation to Rest

He lets me rest in green pastures.

PSALM 23:2

For a field to bear fruit, it must occasionally lie fallow. And for you to be healthy, you must rest. Slow down, and God will heal you. He will bring rest to your mind, to your body, and most of all to your soul. He will lead you to green pastures.

Green pastures were not the natural terrain of Judea. The hills around Bethlehem where David kept his flock were not lush and green. Even today they are white and parched. Any green pasture in Judea is the work of some shepherd. He has cleared the rough, rocky land. Stumps have been torn out, and brush has been burned.

With his own pierced hands, Jesus created a pasture for the soul. He tore out the thorny underbrush of condemnation. He pried loose the huge boulders of sin. In their place he planted seeds of grace and dug ponds of mercy. And he invites us to rest there.

Do you struggle to rest? Do you fear that everything will fall apart if you're not there holding it together?

The Shepherd invites you to rest in his presence, the place of grace he's prepared for you. Accept the invitation. Because rest—that surrender of control—opens your heart to God's peace and healing for your mind, body, and soul. Remember, the one thing you need more than anything else in this life is the one thing that's already been given to you: salvation.

My Scripture of Hope

You have been saved by grace through believing. You did not save yourselves; it was a gift from God.

EPHESIANS 2:8

My Hope to Hold On to and My Worries to Release

God's Promise of Hope to Me

I don't have to save myself—or the world. I can rest in the gift of God's grace.

My Prayer

DAY 78

God Does Not Change

I am Yahweh.

Exodus 6:2 JB

The Israelites considered the name *Yahweh* too holy to be spoken by human lips. Whenever they needed to say *Yahweh*, they substituted the word *Adonai*, which means "Lord." If the name needed to be written, the scribes would take a bath before they wrote it and destroy the pen afterward.

One name God uses for himself is I AM. This name is strikingly close to the Hebrew verb *to be—havah*. It's quite possibly a combination of the present tense form (I am) and the causative tense (I cause to be). *Yahweh*, then, seems to mean "I AM" and "I cause." God is the "One who is" and the "One who causes."

Why is that important? Because we need a big God. And if God is the "One who *is*," then he is an unchanging God.

In a world where everything is changing—from the way we travel and communicate and entertain ourselves down to the very number of hairs on our heads—doesn't your soul long for something steadfast, certain, sure, and unchanging? You have that in God. The same power that raised up mountains, dotted the skies with stars, and raised his own Son to life again is pouring his goodness into your life. *Without fail.* You can trust and believe and follow him because he does not change.

My Scripture of Hope

Every good and perfect gift is from above, coming down from the Father of the heavenly lights, who does not change like shifting shadows.

James 1:17 NIV

My Hope to Hold On to and My Worries to Release

God's Promise of Hope to Me

I can count on God and all his promises. His goodness does not change.

My Prayer

DAY 79

It's Not Too Late to Try Again

We worked hard all night and caught nothing.

LUKE 5:5 NASB

Do you have any wet, worn, empty nets? Do you know the feeling of a sleepless, fishless night? Of course you do. For what have you been casting?

Solvency? "My debt is an anvil around my neck."

Faith? "I want to believe, but . . ."

Healing? "I've been sick for so long."

A happy marriage? "No matter what I do . . ."

"I've worked hard all night and caught nothing."

You've felt what Peter felt. You've sat where Peter sat. And now Jesus is asking you to go fishing. He knows your nets are empty. He knows your heart is weary. He knows you'd like nothing more than to turn your back on the mess and call it a life.

But he urges, "It's not too late to try again."

See if Peter's reply won't help you formulate your own. "I will do as You say and let down the nets" (Luke 5:5 NASB).

Some days are just hard. And sometimes those hard days string together into a stretch that can zap your energy, your strength, and even your faith. Don't let them. When your heart is weary, take a breath, take a nap, and take a knee in prayer. It's not too late to try again. Turn to the One who can restore it all. He is with you. He's got this.

My Scripture of Hope

Don't worry, because I am with you. Don't be afraid, because I am your God. I will make you strong and will help you; I will support you with my right hand that saves you.

ISAIAH 41:10

My Hope to Hold On to and My Worries to Release

God's Promise of Hope to Me

God will give me the strength to try again. He will not let me fall.

My Prayer

DAY 80

Jesus *Is* Coming Back

Always be ready, because you don't know the day your Lord will come.

MATTHEW 24:42

Every person who has ever lived will be present at that final gathering. Every heart that has ever beat. Every mouth that has ever spoken. On that day, you will be surrounded by a sea of people. Rich, poor. Famous, unknown. Kings, bums. Brilliant, demented. All will be present. And all will be looking in one direction. All will be looking at him. Every human being.

"The Son of Man will come again in his great glory" (Matthew 25:31).

You won't look at anyone else. No side glances to see what others are wearing. No whispers about new jewelry or comments about who is present. At this, the greatest gathering in history, you will have eyes for only One—the Son of Man. Wrapped in splendor. Shot through with radiance. Ablaze with light and magnetic in power.

Don't you wonder what it will be like when Jesus returns? The Bible gives a few glimpses, a hint here and there. But the wonder of it all is something we'll have to wait to see. But there's no doubt about it, *we will see*. Because he is coming back. He promised.

My Scripture of Hope

Christ was offered as a sacrifice one time to take away the sins of many people. And he will come a second time, not to offer himself for sin, but to bring salvation to those who are waiting for him.

HEBREWS 9:28

My Hope to Hold On to and My Worries to Release

God's Promise of Hope to Me

Jesus has taken away my sins. And someday he is coming back to take me home with him.

My Prayer

DAY 81

You Are Loved

It is good to . . . sing praises to Your name . . . to declare Your lovingkindness in the morning.
PSALM 92:1–2 NKJV

Listen closely: Jesus' love does not depend on what we do for him. Not at all. In the eyes of the King, you have value simply because you are. You don't have to look nice or perform well. Your value is inborn.

Period.

Think about that for just a minute. You are valuable just because you exist. Not because of what you do or what you have done but simply because you are. Remember that the next time you are left bobbing in the wake of someone's steamboat ambition. Remember that the next time some trickster tries to hang a bargain basement price tag on your self-worth. The next time someone tries to pass you off as a cheap buy, just think about the way Jesus honors you . . . and smile.

I do. I smile because I know I don't deserve love like that. None of us do—but Jesus gives it to us anyway. How wonderful!

You can never repay the price Jesus paid to save you. *Never.* But instead of shrinking under the weight of guilt, let that knowledge do what Jesus intended it to do: set you free. Free of sin and guilt and shame, yes. But also free to be loved, honored, and cherished. Not for what you can give but for who you are. So if the worries of this world ever make you wonder whether his love for you is real, just remember—he died for you!

My Scripture of Hope

Greater love has no one than this: to lay down one's life for one's friends.

JOHN 15:13 NIV

My Hope to Hold On to and My Worries to Release

God's Promise of Hope to Me

Jesus loves me so much that he died for me. And he honors me by calling me his *friend*.

My Prayer

DAY 82

You're Not on Your Own

You have need of endurance, so that when you have done the will of God, you may receive what was promised.
HEBREWS 10:36 NASB

Friends, we have need of endurance. The kind that God gives us. Another description of *enduring* would be "to hang in there until the end" or "to go the distance."

The Brazilians have a great phrase for this. In Portuguese, a person who has the ability to hang in and not give up has *garra. Garra* means "claw." What imagery! A person with *garra* has claws that burrow into the side of the cliff and keep him from falling.

So do the saved. They may get close to the edge; they may even stumble and slide. But they will dig their nails into the rock of God and hang on.

Jesus gives you this assurance. Hang on. He'll make sure you get home.

Life can come at you hard, can't it? You might feel like you're holding on to the edge of the cliff and slipping just a little each moment, but you're not at that edge alone. God is there. Holding you tight with his righteous right hand. Hold tight to him. And if you start to feel like you're slipping, and your worried thoughts whisper, *Is he really there?* remember that God doesn't let go.

My Scripture of Hope

The Lord is faithful and will give you strength and will protect you from the Evil One.

2 Thessalonians 3:3

My Hope to Hold On to and My Worries to Release

God's Promise of Hope to Me

God does not let go. His strength and protection enable me to hold on.

My Prayer

DAY 83

No Loveless Days

I will forgive them for leaving me and will love them freely.

Hosea 14:4

You have never lived a loveless day.

Are you convinced of that? Not one day. Never unloved.

Those times you deserted Christ? He loved you. You hid from him; he came looking for you.

And those occasions you denied Christ? Though you belonged to him, you hung with them, and when his name surfaced, you cursed like a drunken sailor. God let you hear the crowing of conscience and feel the heat of tears. But he never let you go. Your denials cannot diminish his love.

Nor can your doubts. You've had them. You may have them even now. While there is much we cannot know, may never know, can't we be sure of this? Doubts don't separate doubters from God's love.

God's love for you never ends. He never rations. He never runs out. And he never throws his hands up in frustration and cuts off the supply.

So when that day comes—because at one point or another, it comes for us all—when you feel unlovely, unlovable, and unloved, remind yourself that God doesn't quit.

My Scripture of Hope

His unfailing love toward those who fear him is as great as the height of the heavens above the earth.

PSALM 103:11 NLT

My Hope to Hold On to and My Worries to Release

God's Promise of Hope to Me

God's love never fails and never ends. His love *for me* never fails and never ends.

My Prayer

DAY 84

Remember, Jesus Is Still There

Remember Jesus Christ, who was raised from the dead. . . . This is the Good News I preach.

2 TIMOTHY 2:8

In what was perhaps the last letter Paul ever wrote, he urged Timothy to remember.

You can almost picture the old warrior smiling as he wrote the words. "Remember Jesus Christ, who was raised from the dead. . . . This is the Good News I preach" (1 Timothy 2:8).

When times get hard, remember Jesus. When people don't listen, remember Jesus. When tears come, remember Jesus. When disappointment is your bed partner, remember Jesus. When fear pitches its tent in your front yard, when death looms, when anger singes, when shame weighs heavily—remember Jesus.

Remember holiness in tandem with humanity. Remember the sick who were healed by callused hands. Remember the dead who called from the grave with a Galilean accent. Remember the eyes of God that wept human tears.

He is still there. He hasn't left.

Do you remember? Are you still in love with Jesus? Because it's so easy to forget. It's not that you turn away from him . . . you just don't remember to take him with you. Do yourself a favor. Be still and stand before him. Better yet, open your eyes and heart to see him standing before you. And remember, he has promised to stay.

My Scripture of Hope

I will be with you always, even until the end of this age.

MATTHEW 28:20

My Hope to Hold On to and My Worries to Release

God's Promise of Hope to Me

Jesus is with me always. Even when I forget, he remembers me.

My Prayer

It's Your Choice

Accept my teachings and learn from me.
MATTHEW 11:29

It is possible to learn much about God's invitation and never respond to it personally.

Yet his invitation is clear and nonnegotiable.

He gives all and we give him all. Simple and absolute. He is clear in what he asks and clear in what he offers. The choice is up to us. Isn't it incredible that God leaves the choice to us? Think about it. There are many things in life we can't choose. We can't, for example, choose the weather. We can't control the economy.

We can't choose whether or not we are born with a big nose or blue eyes or a lot of hair. We can't even choose how people respond to us.

But we can choose where we spend eternity.

The big choice, God leaves to us. The critical decision is ours.

What are you doing with God's invitation?

How many decisions do you make in a day? A week? A lifetime? So many of them seem important, even crucial. But only one really is. It's not just the choice of a lifetime . . . it's the choice of an eternity. So what's your choice? Will you accept the invitation?

My Scripture of Hope

Come to me, all of you who are tired and have heavy loads, and I will give you rest. Accept my teachings and learn from me, because I am gentle and humble in spirit, and you will find rest for your lives.

Matthew 11:28–29

My Hope to Hold On to and My Worries to Release

God's Promise of Hope to Me

Jesus owns my heart. All he wants is my faith.

My Prayer

DAY 86

A Love Without End

Love never fails.

1 CORINTHIANS 13:8 NIV

Love," Paul says, "never fails."

The verb Paul uses for the word *fail* is used elsewhere to describe the demise of a flower as it falls to the ground, withers, and decays. It carries the meaning of death and abolishment. God's love, says the apostle, will never fall to the ground, wither, and decay. By its nature, it is permanent. It is never abolished.

Love "will last forever" (NLT).
It "never dies" (MSG).
It "never ends" (RSV).
Love "is eternal" (GNT).
God's love "will never come to an end" (NEB).

Governments will fail, but God's love will last. Crowns are temporary, but love is eternal. Your money will run out, but his love never will.

How much time do you spend in fear . . . the fear of running out? Maybe it's running out of money or food. Or perhaps it's running out of time or patience. Or maybe it's even a fear of running out of someone's love. Those things happen. But do you know what doesn't happen? Running out of God's love. So if you've ever worried about that, you can stop now. God's love never runs out.

My Scripture of Hope

Christ's love is greater than anyone can ever know, but I pray that you will be able to know that love. Then you can be filled with the fullness of God.

Ephesians 3:19

My Hope to Hold On to and My Worries to Release

God's Promise of Hope to Me

God loves me more than I'll ever know. His love for me will never fail and never end.

My Prayer

DAY 87

God Loves to Be with You

He gave up his place with God and made himself nothing.
PHILIPPIANS 2:7

Holiday travel. It isn't easy, so why do we do it? Why cram the car trunks and endure the airports? You know the answer. We love to be with the ones we love.

The four-year-old running up the sidewalk into the arms of Grandpa.

The cup of coffee with Mom before the rest of the house awakes.

That moment when everyone is quiet as we hold hands around the table and thank God for family and friends and pumpkin pie.

We love to be with the ones we love.

May I remind you—so does God. He loves to be with the ones he loves. How else do you explain what he did? Between him and us there was a distance—a great span. And he couldn't bear it. He couldn't stand it. So he did something about it.

"He gave up his place . . . and made himself nothing."

God loves to be with you. Let that sink in for a moment. For a lifetime of moments. And he wants you to be with him for always, so God did something about it. Now it's your turn to do something about it, to make sure that you don't miss one moment of eternity with him. Seek him. Accept him. Believe.

My Scripture of Hope

Those who see the Son and believe in him have eternal life, and I will raise them on the last day. This is what my Father wants.

JOHN 6:40

My Hope to Hold On to and My Worries to Release

God's Promise of Hope to Me

God loves to be with me. He sent Jesus to make a way for me to be with him for eternity.

My Prayer

DAY 88

God Is for You

You number my wanderings; put my tears into Your bottle.
Psalm 56:8 NKJV

God knows you. He engraved your name on his hands (Isaiah 49:16) and keeps your tears in a bottle (Psalm 56:8).

God knows you. And he is near you! How far is the shepherd from the sheep (John 10:14)? The branch from the vine (15:5)? That's how far God is from you. He is near. See how these four words look taped to your bathroom mirror: "God is for me" (Psalm 56:9 NKJV).

And his kingdom needs you. The poor need you; the lonely need you; the church needs you . . . the cause of God needs you. You are part of "the overall purpose he is working out in everything and everyone" (Ephesians 1:11 MSG). The kingdom needs you to discover and deploy your unique skill. Use it to make much out of God. Get the word out. God is with us; we are not alone.

God is with you and for you. Does that truth change how you view your struggles? Does it knock your troubles down to size? Does it fill you with a bit more courage, a bit more strength to keep going?

Let it. Let *him*.

My Scripture of Hope

You, dear children, are from God and have overcome them, because the one who is in you is greater than the one who is in the world.

1 John 4:4 NIV

My Hope to Hold On to and My Worries to Release

God's Promise of Hope to Me

God, who is in me, is greater than any trouble I will ever face. He enables me to overcome.

My Prayer

"No More"

The Lord himself will come down from heaven with a loud command.
1 Thessalonians 4:16

Have you ever wondered what that command will be? It will be the inaugural word of heaven. It will be the first audible message most have heard from God. It will be the word that closes one age and opens a new one.

I think I know what the command will be. I could very well be wrong, but I think the command that puts an end to the pains of the earth and initiates the joys of heaven will be two words: "No more."

The King of kings will raise his pierced hand and proclaim, "No more."

The angels will stand, and the Father will speak, "No more."

Every person who lives and who ever lived will turn toward the sky and hear God announce, "No more."

No more loneliness. No more tears. No more death. No more sadness. No more crying. No more pain.

Jesus promised that in this world we would have trouble, but that's not all he promised. He also said he had overcome the world (John 16:33 NIV). There will be an end to the struggle and suffering of this world. For those who believe and trust God, that's good news.

This thing that's wrestling your heart and soul to the ground will not last forever. Something infinitely better waits for you on the other side of this hard life. The end will come. You can count on it.

My Scripture of Hope

I told you these things so that you can have peace in me. In this world you will have trouble, but be brave! I have defeated the world.

John 16:33

My Hope to Hold On to and My Worries to Release

God's Promise of Hope to Me

Jesus has already defeated the evil of this world. My troubles will not last forever. I will claim victory!

My Prayer

DAY 90

An Eye Toward the Sky

Therefore keep watch, because you do not know the day or the hour.

MATTHEW 25:13 NIV

A tourist visited a beautiful mansion in Switzerland. He was stunned by the gardens, not a weed anywhere. Seeing the gardener, the tourist asked, "How long have you worked here?"

"Twenty years," came the answer.

"Does the owner live here?"

"No. In all these years, I've only seen him four times."

"He must be grateful. You tend the grounds as if you expect him to return tomorrow."

"Oh, no. I tend them as if I expect him to return today."[1]

Let's do likewise. For all we know, our Master will do just that. He is the God of divine interruptions. Holy surprises. Who could have imagined God living on earth? But he came. Who could've imagined God hanging on a cross? But he died. Who could have imagined the empty tomb? But he rose from the dead. He intervenes in mighty and miraculous ways.

He has before. He will again.

In the meantime, keep an eye toward the sky. Live in such a way that Christ will find you faithfully looking for him.

> If Christ returned in this moment—so suddenly that you dropped this very book you're reading—would you be ready for him? Decide today to live with an eye toward the sky so that God will look at you and say, "You did well, child."

My Scripture of Hope

You did well. You are a good and loyal servant. . . . Come and share my joy with me.

MATTHEW 25:21

My Hope to Hold On to and My Worries to Release

God's Promise of Hope to Me

When I am faithful with the small things of life, God will entrust to me the greater things of his kingdom. He will share his joy with me.

My Prayer

Promise Quick-Reference Guide

DAY 1

1 JOHN 1:5

Today's Promise: *One day, darkness will end. Tears will end. Struggles and troubles will end. There will be only God's light, love, joy, and peace. And I will live in it forever . . . with God.*

DAY 2

PSALM 19:7 NKJV

Today's Promise: *I can see the power of God in this world. I can know that he is real and at work by the witness of his creation.*

DAY 3

2 CORINTHIANS 4:17 NLT

Today's Promise: *The struggles and troubles of this world will soon be over. God—his love, his goodness, and my life with him—will last forever.*

DAY 4

HEBREWS 8:12 RSV

Today's Promise: *When I take my sins to God, he not only forgives; he also forgets. I can forgive myself and forget those sins too.*

DAY 5

1 JOHN 4:10

Today's Promise: *There is nowhere I can go where God's love will not find me.*

DAY 6

JEREMIAH 1:5

Today's Promise: *I am God's custom design. He will enable me to live out the purpose he has assigned me—a purpose that will please him and bring joy to me.*

DAY 7

PSALM 23:3 NKJV

Today's Promise: *God sent Jesus so I can be with him. When I put my faith in Jesus, he makes me right with God, and I can leave my sins and guilt at the cross.*

DAY 8

JOHN 20:25

Today's Promise: *God is able to do the impossible. He keeps every promise he makes.*

DAY 9

REVELATION 1:5

Today's Promise: *God's grace doesn't depend on me meeting a set of expectations. It depends on his perfect love.*

DAY 10

JOHN 1:3

Today's Promise: *The miracles of God are all around me. They declare that he is real and very, very near.*

DAY 11

JEREMIAH 31:34 NKJV

Today's Promise: *I can let go of my past. It is gone. Christ has made me new!*

DAY 12

PSALM 31:19

Today's Promise: *God has prepared a place for me with him. It will be more wonderful than anything I could ever imagine.*

DAY 13

PHILIPPIANS 4:4 NKJV

Today's Promise: *God's love and goodness are with me always. He invites me into his house to live with him forever.*

DAY 14

EXODUS 16:4

Today's Promise: *God knows what I need, and I can trust him to meet all my needs.*

DAY 15

MATTHEW 24:36

Today's Promise: *Jesus will come back for me. He will rescue me and take me to be with him for eternity.*

DAY 16

PSALM 141:1

Today's Promise: *God walks with me. He listens to my prayers, and he answers them . . . perfectly.*

DAY 17

PSALM 103:11

Today's Promise: *God's love for me cannot be measured. I can't lose it, and I don't have to earn it. It is mine simply because I am his.*

DAY 18

REVELATION 5:10 NIV

Today's Promise: *Jesus has a place for me, not just in his kingdom, but at his table. My true self and my destiny are found in him.*

DAY 19

PHILIPPIANS 3:8

Today's Promise: *Jesus calls me his friend.*

DAY 20

PSALM 139:8 NIV

Today's Promise: *The miracles of God cannot be counted. He is constantly at work in this world.*

DAY 21

NUMBERS 23:19

Today's Promise: *Only God is God. He will always do what he says he will do. I can trust the ending to him.*

DAY 22

JOHN 14:1 NIV

Today's Promise: *I will look to Jesus. He created my faith, and he will continue working to perfect it.*

DAY 23

ISAIAH 45:18

Today's Promise: *God invites me to turn my troubles over to him. I can trust him. He will not let me down.*

DAY 24

PSALM 119:65

Today's Promise: *God puts eternal instants—priceless moments—into my life. And he invites me to stand with him there on holy ground.*

DAY 25

PSALM 139:14 NKJV

Today's Promise: *I am no accident. I was fearfully and wonderfully made by God, in the image of God.*

DAY 26

PSALM 105:2 NKJV

Today's Promise: *God's love for me is sure and certain. I can rest in it even as I wait to see his goodness at work in my life.*

DAY 27

1 TIMOTHY 6:12

Today's Promise: *Christ has promised me life—an eternal life with him. He always keeps his promises.*

DAY 28

LUKE 15:32

Today's Promise: *God will not leave me lost and wandering. He will search until he finds me. He will hold me close to his heart.*

DAY 29

ROMANS 15:13 TLB

Today's Promise: *Jesus is the light of the world. When I follow him, he lights up my path and chases away the darkness. He is my light, all my life.*

DAY 30

ISAIAH 53:10 NIV

Today's Promise: *God sent his Son because he loves me. Jesus gave up his life because he loves me. Because of the cross, I can live in that love forever.*

DAY 31

LUKE 18:27

Today's Promise: *God can do anything. And he has promised to do good things for me.*

DAY 32

1 CHRONICLES 16:11 NIV

Today's Promise: *God shines his light into my life. He is my strong Father who chases away the shadows and the darkness.*

DAY 33

1 JOHN 5:4

Today's Promise: *No matter what happens in this world, I have victory in Jesus. I have already won the best possible reward . . . for eternity.*

DAY 34

JOHN 16:13 NIV

Today's Promise: *I can know God's heart even when I don't know his plans. And his heart is filled with love and good plans for me.*

DAY 35

MATTHEW 11:28

Today's Promise: *Jesus knows me personally. He invites me—personally—to follow him.*

DAY 36

JAMES 4:14

Today's Promise: *Death has no power over me. Jesus has taken away its sting. I don't have to worry about what comes next, because Jesus is already there waiting for me.*

DAY 37

ACTS 1:11 NASB

Today's Promise: *God is merciful and good. Because Jesus rose again, I have the hope—the promise—of eternity with him.*

DAY 38

ROMANS 9:25 MSG

Today's Promise: *God loves me. I can count on his love. He will not stop loving me.*

DAY 39

1 PETER 3:18 NIV

Today's Promise: *I can rest in God. He is my salvation.*

DAY 40

PSALM 23:1

Today's Promise: *My God, my Shepherd, watches over me. He will never leave or abandon me. I can be content because he is all I truly need.*

DAY 41

HEBREWS 2:17 MSG

Today's Promise: *Because I believe, I am a citizen of God's kingdom. I belong to God's family.*

DAY 42

PSALM 117:2 MSG

Today's Promise: *I am saved by God's mercy and grace. No one can snatch me away from him.*

DAY 43

JOHN 3:16 NKJV

Today's Promise: *Christ died to save me from sin and give me a new life with him. His wounds have healed me.*

DAY 44

JOHN 19:30

Today's Promise: *When I remain in Jesus, he remains in me. He will help me not only endure but thrive.*

DAY 45

PSALM 103:4

Today's Promise: *God can do anything. He can—and will—forgive my every mistake, blunder, and sin. Why? Because he loves me more than I could ever imagine.*

DAY 46

1 CORINTHIANS 4:5

Today's Promise: *God sees my efforts. He doesn't forget the good I try to do. And one day, He will praise me for it. Personally.*

DAY 47

GALATIANS 3:27

Today's Promise: *God sees Christ in me. I am clothed in his spotless robe of righteousness.*

DAY 48

PHILIPPIANS 2:10

Today's Promise: *When I serve others, I serve Jesus. He will see and bless me.*

DAY 49

JOHN 10:15 NIV

Today's Promise: *Jesus knows me, and I can know him. He will shepherd me through this life and into forever with him.*

DAY 50

MARK 13:26 NIV

Today's Promise: *God will lift me up above the struggles of this world. He will give me a firm place to stand while I watch and wait for Jesus' return.*

DAY 51

HEBREWS 12:6

Today's Promise: *God is Lord over all. He made me, and I am his; he disciplines me out of love.*

DAY 52

PHILIPPIANS 3:8

Today's Promise: *Christ sacrificed himself for me. For me. To set me free from my sins forever.*

DAY 53

DEUTERONOMY 7:8

Today's Promise: *God lavishes his love on me. He calls me his child. And that is who I am!*

DAY 54

MATTHEW 22:2 NKJV

Today's Promise: *Jesus sacrificed himself so that I could come to the wedding, pure, spotless, and without fault.*

DAY 55

HEBREWS 2:8 MSG

Today's Promise: *God chose me to be his child. Even before the world was made, he had a plan to rescue me.*

DAY 56

GENESIS 3:8 MSG

Today's Promise: *God searches for those who are lost and wandering. He searches until he finds them. If I wander, God will search until he finds me.*

DAY 57

ROMANS 8:27

Today's Promise: *It's not all up to me. The Holy Spirit is with me to help me . . . forever.*

DAY 58

GALATIANS 5:26 MSG

Today's Promise: *I am fearfully and wonderfully made by God himself. When I do what he created me to do, I make God smile.*

DAY 59

1 CORINTHIANS 13:4, 7 NIV

Today's Promise: *I am loved by God. Perfectly and completely. His love will never fail me.*

DAY 60

1 JOHN 4:19

Today's Promise: *God chose me to be his child. It's what he wanted, and it pleases him.*

DAY 61

PSALM 103:10

Today's Promise: *I don't have to be perfect to be perfectly loved by God.*

DAY 62

ISAIAH 53:5

Today's Promise: *I can trust God to forgive my sins. He will make me clean again.*

DAY 63

EXODUS 35:35 NIV

Today's Promise: *I was handcrafted by God. He has purpose for me and for my life.*

DAY 64

1 JOHN 3:1

Today's Promise: *God's love for me is perfect and complete. I have no reason to fear. I am safe inside God's love.*

DAY 65

JOHN 3:31

Today's Promise: *Jesus understands my struggles. He's faced them all too. And he knows just how to help me.*

DAY 66

HEBREWS 10:22

Today's Promise: *Jesus came to make a way for me to be with God. He is the only way to God. When I choose to follow him, he leads me to eternal life.*

DAY 67

REVELATION 21:15–16 NLT

Today's Promise: *There is room for me in God's house. Jesus is already there, preparing a place just for me.*

DAY 68

GALATIANS 3:13

Today's Promise: *In Christ, I am fully forgiven and set free from my sins. I am covered and clothed in God's rich grace.*

DAY 69

ISAIAH 55:1

Today's Promise: *God's invitation is for me. And when I accept, I become his own child.*

DAY 70

MATTHEW 1:23 NKJV

Today's Promise: *Jesus knows and notices me. He came to give me life in all its fullness!*

DAY 71

MATTHEW 12:18

Today's Promise: *God sent his Son to save me, to take away my sins, and to give me a new life in him. That is real love, and that is how God loves me.*

DAY 72

REVELATION 21:1, 3–4

Today's Promise: *One day, I will walk on streets of gold. I will live where there is no darkness. And I will look into the face of God.*

DAY 73

ROMANS 5:5 NKJV

Today's Promise: *I am God's child. I don't have to be afraid—I belong to him.*

DAY 74

ZEPHANIAH 3:17 NKJV

Today's Promise: *God delights in me. His love will never fail me.*

DAY 75

REVELATION 21:5 NKJV

Today's Promise: *One day, everything will be better than I could ever imagine. No sorrow, death, or pain. Only joy and wonder and God. Forever.*

DAY 76

1 CORINTHIANS 15:51–52 NKJV

Today's Promise: *I am sealed by God with his Holy Spirit. I am guaranteed an inheritance in his kingdom.*

DAY 77

PSALM 23:2

Today's Promise: *I don't have to save myself—or the world. I can rest in the gift of God's grace.*

DAY 78

EXODUS 6:2 JB

Today's Promise: *I can count on God and all his promises. His goodness does not change.*

DAY 79

LUKE 5:5 NASB

Today's Promise: *God will give me the strength to try again. He will not let me fall.*

DAY 80

MATTHEW 24:42

Today's Promise: *Jesus has taken away my sins. And someday he is coming back to take me home with him.*

DAY 81

PSALM 92:1–2 NKJV

Today's Promise: *Jesus loves me so much that he died for me. And he honors me by calling me his friend.*

DAY 82

HEBREWS 10:36 NASB

Today's Promise: *God does not let go. His strength and protection enable me to hold on.*

DAY 83

HOSEA 14:4

Today's Promise: *God's love never fails and never ends. His love for me never fails and never ends.*

DAY 84

2 TIMOTHY 2:8

Today's Promise: *Jesus is with me always. Even when I forget, he remembers me.*

DAY 85

MATTHEW 11:29

Today's Promise: *Jesus owns my heart. All he wants is my faith.*

DAY 86

1 CORINTHIANS 13:8 NIV

Today's Promise: *God loves me more than I'll ever know. His love for me will never fail and never end.*

DAY 87

PHILIPPIANS 2:7

Today's Promise: *God loves to be with me. He sent Jesus to make a way for me to be with him for eternity.*

DAY 88

PSALM 56:8 NKJV

Today's Promise: *God, who is in me, is greater than any trouble I will ever face. He enables me to overcome.*

DAY 89

1 THESSALONIANS 4:16

Today's Promise: *Jesus has already defeated the evil of this world. My troubles will not last forever. I will claim victory!*

DAY 90

MATTHEW 25:13 NIV

Today's Promise: *When I am faithful with the small things of life, God will entrust to me the greater things of his kingdom. He will share his joy with me.*

Notes

Day 15: Know Where You're Headed

1. Mark Hitchcock, *The End: Everything You'll Want to Know About the Apocalypse* (Tyndale, 2018), 4–5.

Day 34: In His Hands

1. Revelation 1:8; 4:8; 11:17; 15:3; 16:7; 16:14; 19:15; 21:22.

Day 47: Who God Sees

1. "My Hope Is Built on Nothing Less," by Edward Mote, 1834; public domain.

Day 67: God Has Room for You

1. Randy Alcorn, *Heaven: A Comprehensive Guide to Everything the Bible Says About Our Eternal Home* (Tyndale, 2011), 242.

Day 90: An Eye Toward the Sky

1. Denis Lyle, *Countdown to Apocalypse* (Ambassador, 1999), 21.

About the Author

Since entering the ministry in 1978, Max Lucado has served churches in Miami, Florida; Rio de Janeiro, Brazil; and San Antonio, Texas. He currently serves as the teaching minister of Oak Hills Church in San Antonio. He is the recipient of the 2021 ECPA Pinnacle Award for his outstanding contribution to the publishing industry and society at large. He is America's bestselling inspirational author with more than 150 million products in print.

Visit his website at MaxLucado.com
Facebook.com/MaxLucado
Instagram.com/MaxLucado
X.com/MaxLucado
Youtube.com/MaxLucadoOfficial
The Max Lucado Encouraging Word Podcast